SO-BWV-545

Japan--Land and Men

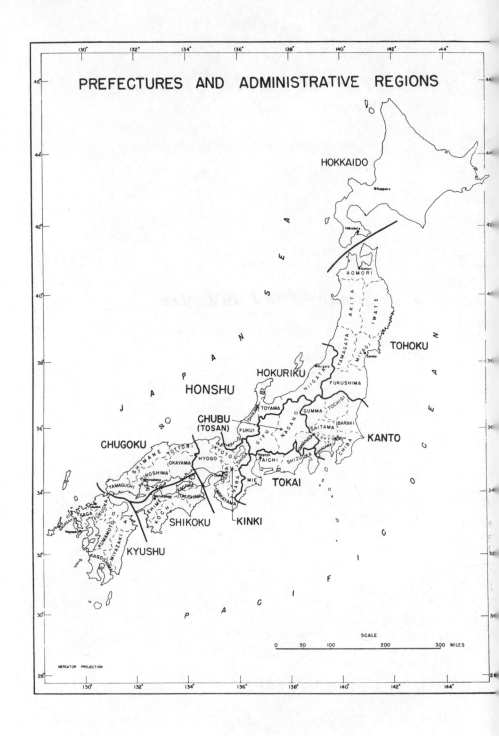

PREFECTURES AND ADMINISTRATIVE REGIONS

Japan--Land and Men

An Account of the Japanese Land Reform
Program — 1945 - 51

by

LAURENCE I. HEWES, JR.

Agricultural Economist
Bureau of Reclamation, Denver, Colorado

Formerly, Land Reform Specialist
Allied Occupation of Japan, Tokyo

GREENWOOD PRESS, PUBLISHERS
WESTPORT, CONNECTICUT

Library of Congress Cataloging in Publication Data

Hewes, Laurence Ilsley, 1902–
    Japan—land and men.

    Reprint of the ed. published by Iowa State College
Press, Ames, Iowa.
    Bibliography: p.
    1. Land reform—Japan. 2. Peasantry—Japan.
I. Title.
[HD915.H4 1974]   333.1'0952   74–8262
ISBN 0–8371–7574–7

Originally published in 1955 by The Iowa State College Press,
Ames, Iowa

Reprinted with the permission of The Iowa State University
Press

Reprinted in 1974 by Greenwood Press,
a division of Williamhouse-Regency Inc.

Library of Congress Catalog Card Number 74-8262

ISBN 0-8371-7574-7

Printed in the United States of America

AUTHOR'S NOTE AND ACKNOWLEDGMENT

This book relates the story of the Japanese Land Reform Program against a background of the history and sociology of agrarian Japan. In an earlier work I have given a more technical account of the Program.[*] The present study amplifies the historical and sociological aspects of the Reform, particularly through the material given in Chapters 3 and 4. The principal sources of these chapters were:

1. Translations by Aston and Chamberlain of those ancient Japanese books, the *Kojiki* and the *Nihongi*.

2. Voluminous historical material in the form of addresses and essays appearing in *Transactions of the Asiatic Society of Japan*.

3. Numerous articles and books by the noted Japanese historical economist, Enjiro Honjo.

4. The treasure house of documentary historical material contained in *The Documents of Iriki*, so painstakingly prepared by the late Kanichi Asakawa of Yale University.

5. The systematic historical account of Japan's development by Yaseburo Takekoshi, *The Economic Aspects of the History of the Civilization of Japan*.

6. Sir George B. Sansom's *Japan, A Short Cultural History*, which remains as the classical work on this subject.

7. Articles by numerous Japanese economists and historians in the Kyoto University *Economic Review*. A complete set of all copies of this fine journal were kindly presented to me by Dr. Kenji Maki of Kyoto University.

8. Mr. E. Herbert Norman's *Japan's Emergence as a Modern State*. I found this work particularly helpful to an understanding of the period just preceding and subsequent to the Meiji Revolution.

9. The SCAP publication *Farm Tenancy in Japan*, which was prepared by Wolf I. Ladejinsky.

Of course, all of us who write about rural Japan owe a debt to the late John Embree for his definitive work on the Japanese rural village, *Suye Mura*. With the permission of the University of Chicago Press, I have followed Embree's analysis and terminology in parts of Chapter 2.

---

[*]*Japanese Land Reform Program* (Tokyo: General Headquarters Supreme Commander for the Allied Powers, Natural Resources Section, Report No. 127, 1950).

I wish to thank The Macmillan Company for their permission to use several quotations from the writings of Lafcadio Hearn, and Marshall Jones and Company for permission to use in Chapter 7 quotations from Masaharu Anezaki's *Art, Life, and Nature in Japan.*

I am indebted to Clyde Mitchell of the University of Nebraska, Philip Raup of the University of Minnesota, John Timmons of Iowa State College, and Joseph Ackerman of the Farm Foundation for their kind efforts to secure publication of this book, and to the Iowa State College Press through which publication was effected.

Laurence I. Hewes, Jr.

Denver, Colorado
May, 1955

CONTENTS

ILLUSTRATIONS

Chapter 1

THE SETTING

OUR jeep halted at the crest of the mountains; the drive had been long and difficult up the narrow rough roads from Lake Biwa. Pausing, we gazed down the rugged slopes and canyons toward Kyoto, the ancient capital. The panorama we viewed was no scene of mountain wilderness but a pattern of carefully designed, intensively cultivated fields. From above, the terraced rice paddies descended in irregularly shaped patches. Tiny terraced fields formed a landscape in shades of the vivid green of newly planted rice down the mountain sides. No gorge or canyon was too steep, no hill too abrupt to halt their graceful curving overlay, transforming the scene from mountain vastness to pastoral intimacy.

The roads, built not originally for wheeled vehicles, but as a passageway for the toiling feet of generations, were jolting torture to ride over. At every hairpin turn, burdened farm men and women stood aside to permit our passage. Their poised loads signified their common occupation – great bundles of straw, leaves, and twigs were being carried to the homestead for use as compost for the fields or for fuel in the home. These had all been gleaned in the most painstaking fashion from the neighboring wooded area.

The ancient highway narrowed to enter the teeming heighborhood – clusters of tiny farmsteads, the *buraku,* which made up the village of Oharame. Like all Japanese villages, Oharame is a collection of neighboring hamlets and all the surrounding tilled fields together with the adjoining forest land whose tribute of compost and firewood is an essential part of the village economy. The village is very old, for this part of Japan has been settled for centuries. Traditionally, the stalwart men of Oharame have been selected as pallbearers for the funerals of the Japanese emperors. So the fields and farmsteads of Oharame are not the crude achievement of a transitory settlement nor is the village a result of recent agrarian development. On the contrary, it is the manifestation of a very old and complex civilization. Strange and primitive to Western eyes, Oharame and its fields nevertheless represent civilization – civilization in different terms and in unfamiliar patterns, but in the essentials of an established social order, an orderly development of man's relation to natural resources, still a valid instance of a completely matured culture.

1

Origins of Japanese Farming System

The tiny terraces, so green with the young rice plants, and the
maze of associated irrigation and drainage ways were painfully laid
by human hands long before the American continent was discovered.
The intricate arrangements of landed property relations and methods
of sharing produce from these fields were subjects for discourses by
scholars and for judicial decisions by jurists before many precepts of
British common law had even been formulated. Near Oharame, Kyoto,
the former capital of Japan, was the cultural flowering of a vital
social organization in the twelfth century. The economic base which
made all this possible was agriculture and predominantly rice culture.
Thus land and its cultivation lay close to the heart of a colorful and
dynamic social process from which modern Japan with its many problems emerges. Through centuries Japanese peasants, the paddy
fields, and the rice crop were an essential core from which spread
law, politics, poetry, drama, as well as all the other external manifestations which together spell Japan.

The *Kojiki* is one of the earliest written Japanese historical records.
Its account of the founding of the Japanese nation by Jimmu Tenno,
about 660 B.C., relates that a brother of the sun-goddess in a wild
orgy tore down the balks between paddy fields. Almost without exception, later historical accounts discuss at great length agrarian problems, landholding systems, methods of dividing the rice crop, and
similar agrarian matters. One then pictures the Japanese as having
engaged from the earliest times in agriculture and primarily in cultivation of paddy field rice.

Vague conjectures of Japanese origins first locate these extraordinary people in the northern part of the southern main island of
Kyushu. Later, moving north, they were well established by the ninth
century throughout southern Honshu, the central island, with an elaborate capital at Nara. From this point and later from Kyoto the detailed history of Japan unfolds.

Japanese clans migrated slowly from southern Honshu, subduing
the rugged mountainous remainder of Honshu and the equally rugged
islands of Shikoku and Hokkaido by force of arms. The new areas
were first gradually brought under the central authority of a kingdom.
Settlement largely involved imposition of military authority and open-
ing up new agricultural lands. Thus methods of cultivation and
systems of land tenure, developed at the center of authority, spread,
in a period of about 700 years, to all the main islands, except the
northern island of Hokkaido. The conquest of Japan by the Japanese
was thus a process of extending to all parts of the territory rather
uniform practices of rice agriculture and a system of land tenure conceived to be suited to it.

Very early property records on the island of Kyushu indicate, as a
general rule, the characteristic cultivation of small fields. This may
have been due to physical limitations resulting from the laborious task

of carving level paddy fields out of a rugged terrain by hand labor. It
is also possible that the inching backward of the northern frontier and
the gradual conquest, over the centuries, of remaining islands derived
part of its expansive dynamism from population pressure.At all events,
the agrarian settlement appears to have been characterized by the
gradual spread of an individually operated, small-scale, paddy field
system of agriculture. This conjecture is sustained by the remarkable uniformity throughout Japan of patterns of cultivation for staple
crops. Exceptions were found in parts of northern Honshu and on the
island of Hokkaido, where more extensive farming patterns exist.

There are many gaps in the proof that diminutive fields cultivated
by single families have always characterized Japanese agriculture.
Nevertheless, evidence of the prevalence of other forms at any time
is almost completely lacking. There appear to be no grounds for a
belief that the present system derived from an earlier more extensive
system or that any form of communal cultivation ever existed. This
evidence constitutes perhaps the chief grounds for belief that for over
1,500 years prevailing patterns of Japanese cultivation have remained
more or less constant. This system is uniquely distinct from the
cultivation patterns of European feudalism out of which modern Western landed property institutions have developed.

Under the cloak of appearance, rural Oharame is a segment of an
agrarian culture, of methods of cultivation, and of land tenure relations which have matured through centuries of Japanese life and are
truly representative of much of rural Japan. While in times past,
change came to little Oharame, it occurred, with few exceptions, in
the slow tempo of rural time and in pastoral rhythms. Of injustice
and of suffering Oharame has seen much – inevitable consequences,
perhaps, where fields are so tiny, disaster so frequent, and so many
must share the produce of so little land. But the changes which modern life has brought to the people of Oharame have always tended to
complicate their lives and to increase their hardships. Not all have
suffered alike; indeed, some have not suffered at all, and a few,
perhaps, have prospered.

Probably no one knows exactly how or when the difficulties began
which now beset so many farmers. Perhaps the origins lie hidden in
the warp and woof of centuries of gradual cultural development;
perhaps it lies in the conflicts between this development and more
recent influences that appeared as Japan became a modern empire.
Certain it is, the farm people of Oharame were caught in a dilemma
from which unaided they could not escape.

Population and Land Use

The dilemma of Oharame is the dilemma of all of rural Japan –
too many people, too little land. For Japan's islands are rugged, with
little space for farms. Except for a few broad coastal plains like the
Kanto, the Yamashiro, and the Shonai, the four main islands of the

Japanese Archipelago are extremely mountainous volcanic masses.
In the narrow floors of short valleys and on adjacent hillsides, centuries of toil have carved out thousands of acres of farm land terraces.
Even so, the soil here has several deficiencies. Of recent volcanic
origin, poor in texture, in part excessively porous, in other places
badly drained, the soils of Japan, naturally low in available mineral
elements and in organic matter, are continuously leached by the heavy
rainfall of the monsoon climate. In order to practice cultivation with
any hope at all of success, continuous heavy application of fertilizer
and organic matter is necessary.

Today there are between fifteen and sixteen million acres of agricultural land in Japan, and this land is cultivated by about six and a
half million farm families. The average unit consists of a little less
than two and a half acres. In northern Honshu the farms are a little
larger. These northern units raise the average somewhat, thus con-
cealing very much smaller sizes prevalent in the more populous
districts of southern Honshu and the island of Kyushu. On the west
central coast of Honshu, on the shore of the Sea of Japan is the village
or *mura* of Yuwaku Dani in Ishikawa prefecture. In 1947, there were
134 farm families in this village which had a total farming area of
about 275 acres – just a little over two acres per farm. In contrast
is Higashi Wasada Mura near the port city, Beppu, of Oita prefecture,
on the island of Kyushu, where 519 families cultivate 768 acres, less
than an acre and a half per farm. The extremes of small Japanese
cultivation are found in southern Honshu on the Pacific Ocean side of
the island. It is from this area, which includes Okayama, Hiroshima,
and Yamaguchi prefectures, that most of the Japanese immigrants
came to the United States. Ono Mura, of Seki Gun (county) in Hiroshima prefecture, has 1,005 farm families who farm a total of 550
acres. Fortunately, Ono Mura is on the Inland Sea so over 700 of its
farm families are able to supplement their farm income with fishing.
But for all Japan, physical limitations of the islands plus population
increase plus historical development have combined to create a pattern of overly small farms from which there appears to be no escape.
It seems probable that Japanese farms will continue to be operated
indefinitely on their present or on a gradually diminishing scale.

In spite of such handicaps the Japanese farmer is a remarkable
producer. Of course, the principal crop is paddy field rice, to which
about half the land is dedicated. The balance of the land is in upland
crops, of which wheat, barley, rye, millet, sweet potatoes, and white
potatoes are the principal items. Yields per acre of rice are among
the highest in the world and considerably exceed production in several
other more fertile and suitable regions. Due largely to the energy and
skill of Japanese farmers, a nation over eighty million people today
receive 80 per cent of their staple food requirements from domestic
production. Japanese farmers have a rate of rice production from 50
to 200 per cent higher per acre than farmers of any other Asian
country.

It is easy to become enthusiastic over the indomitable quiet courage of the Japanese farmers. It is they and they alone whose bent backs and busy hands have supported for centuries almost without assistance the superstructure of an entire nation and its associated culture. Their existence has been essential to the development of art, letters, and government. They were indispensable factors to creation of an empire. Yet all the while their lot has been an endless scroll of unremitting toil and hardship. Every year from May until October they toil knee-deep in mud and water to bring forth the rice. Every year from October until May they painstakingly repair paddy fields, till them, and bring leaves, twigs, and all manner of compost to replenish organic matter in the soil. Then, in late fall they plant winter wheat or barley for a second crop which is harvested just before the young rice crop is set out.

On the west coast of Honshu is fascinating Shimane prefecture where in places wet marshy plains meet precipitous mountains. Heavy soil and poor drainage make necessary a method of cultivation called *taka-une*. By this device, since the boggy fields will not drain, the soil is banked up from the floor of the paddy field into dykes or broad banks about 6 inches to a foot above the water. Each dyke appears to be about 24 inches wide. On the top of these dykes a cover crop of clover is planted. As planting season approaches, the dykes are broken down to a level surface. This practice is supposed to counteract the acidity of the soil and increase fertility. But the labor which the operation requires is fantastic. In areas where *taka-une* is necessary they say that only strong young women find husbands. No matter how beautiful or graceful otherwise, feminine fragility is not a virtue in the *taka-une* districts.

In Japan and probably in most of Asia, the margin of safety is low. When one is totally dependent on the income represented by produce from less than two and a half acres there is nothing to spare for plant disease, insect pests, drought, flood, or other disasters. Yet widespread disaster is so commonplace in Japan as to constitute a constant hazard in cultivation. In the early summer of 1947, floods destroyed crops through a wide area in the Tohoku region of northern Honshu. Toward the end of that summer a flood of the Tone River ravaged thousands of acres and caused terrible damage to life and property in Chiba and Saitama prefectures near Tokyo. Just a little later, heavy rains at the time of harvest caused much harvestable rice to "lodge" (i.e., fall down) in the paddies of the Ishikawa peninsula. In 1948, widespread floods occurred in Miyagi prefecture on the northwest coast of Honshu. In addition to floods and earthquakes, avalanches and tidal waves frequently cause great damage to the countryside. These are natural processes under whose portent every Japanese farm family starts and ends each day of its existence. An American farmer perhaps plants his crop with some doubt as to the amount of harvest and its price. The Japanese farmer plants a crop not knowing if he will live to harvest it or even if there will be a crop.

Women work too, Niigata prefecture. (Courtesy, U. S. Army.)

Night soil, human feces and urine, is the common source of animal manure in Japan. Its constant application to growing crops is essential to successful production. Since the Japanese farmer has no mechanical aid in this operation, he must carry this fertilizer in buckets from storage pits to his fields and there ladle it on each plant with a long-handled dipper. During the growing season, in the extremes of Japan's near-tropical summer, pleasant-appearing countrysides everywhere exhale the odor of sewage. An adjunct of agriculture is the constant procession of night-soil carriers from the cities. On every main highway, every rural road, and every byway, the slow-paced wagons transporting night soil move ceaselessly, drawn sometimes by draught animals, cattle or horses, more frequently by human beings – two men, often a man and a woman, sometimes by three or four people. Throughout the long past and under conditions likely to prevail in the future, there has been and can be no cessation of this eternal struggle to maintain the fertility of Japan's soil. For the Japanese, who are extremely sensitive to beauty and ugliness, night soil and its constant handling are hateful yet essential requirements of survival and must therefore be stoically accepted as such.

Chapter 2

THE JAPANESE RURAL VILLAGE

JAPANESE rural life and the bulk of its agrarian economy are
centered in thousands of rural villages. These communities are
tucked away in the folds of the mountains, scattered along the narrow courses of rushing rivers, or dotted over the plains. Indeed,
to many visitors, artists and writers, vivid memories of the Japanese
village, its quaintness, charm, and pleasant natural setting constitute
an impression which colors their entire remembrance of Japan. Nor
is this impression altogether false, for these communities are representative of a very large segment of Japanese life and economy. Some
villages are large, like Ebetsu on the island of Hokkaido, with 30,000
people one-third of whom are farmers; others are medium-sized like
Nobuta in Nagano in north central Honshu, with 659 households of which
607 are farmers. One could go on; there is Nikaido Village in ancient
Nara, with 2,086 families over half of whom are cultivators in contrast to small Tatsichi Village, also in Nara, with 304 families and
500 acres of cultivated land. Thus villages range from about 1,000 to
25,000 inhabitants, and the proportion of farmers appears to be larger
among the smaller villages. Farmer and non-farmer inhabitants of
rural Japan total more than half the national population. The majority
of these dwell in villages. So a very large population lives out its
existence within the unique physical and social confines of one or another of the thousands of rural villages scattered over the hillsides,
mountains, and plains, among ravines, along river courses or beside
bays and inlets of the sea.

Despite great variation of physical location, many aspects of these
villages are similar. True, there are differences, as tile roofs of
Okayama contrast with prevalent thatch roofs of the Kanto Plain, and
partly mud-walled houses of some southern districts differ from
wooden-sided dwellings in the Tohoku region of northeastern Japan.
But the lines and design are all similar. Some villages radiate from
a common center, while others extend like beads on a necklace along
a narrow river course. Sometimes, where mountains and plains
merge, compact hillside settlements change with the ampler space to
wider and more open types. Even so, the purpose and function are
similar and familiarity with features of one village provides a common
denominator of understanding for those of many others.

Scattered farmhouse clusters or *buraku,* which collectively comprise

Rural scene on the island of Shikoku. Several hamlets or *buraku* make up a single village.
(Courtesy, U. S. Army.)

the village, are islands in a surrounding sea of tilled fields which
make up the village farm land. Beyond are the hills or mountains
whose forested and bush-grown slopes provide the associated forest
land from which come the leaves and grass for compost as well as for
fuel wood and charcoal. Typically, ten to twenty smaller *buraku*, varying in size from four to twenty or more homesteads, each separated
from the other by an eighth to a quarter of a mile, constitute a village.
Usually, one of the *buraku*, somewhat larger than the others, serves
as a trading center; here are located shops, administrative buildings,
the railroad station, and the village school. In his study of Suye Mura
in Kumamoto prefecture, Embree grouped *buraku* into occupational
types, distinguishing between paddy field, upland field, and shopkeeper
hamlets.[1]

Generally, with the increase of highway traffic, the central *buraku*
of the village is located astride the principal road or highway. Narrow
farm roads, branching from the main road, provide communication
among the several *buraku*. Still beyond, narrower footpaths and trails
form a network that gives access to complicated patterns of farm
fields and ditches. Thus fields, ditches, paths, trails, highways, forest
land, tilled fields, and *buraku* of varying size and occupational purpose
make up the physical apparatus of the Japanese village.

Pausing for a moment to view the village scene one is soon aware
of an intense human busyness on all sides. There is no such thing,
during daylight hours, anyway, as an empty stretch of road, or fields
devoid of life. On every road, or path, in almost every direction,
someone is in motion. As one observes more closely, it seems that
there are people everywhere, all doing something, all engaged in some
task. There is very little real noise. The whole peopled scene seems
startlingly silent. Yet in the aggregate one feels that the principal
theme should be a buzz or hum of activity. There is much coming and
going, sometimes by bicycle, sometimes afoot. A farmer drags a
two-wheeled cart and his two daughters help push it while a young man
returns from the fields dextrously riding his bicycle on the narrow
ridge between two paddy fields. In the middle foreground a young
mother with infant on her back stands for a moment talking to another
woman; farther off, a three-wheeled cargo motorcycle stirs the dust
of the highway, while unheralded, a very old woman suddenly emerges
from a steep hillside path enormously burdened with bundles of twigs
and leaves. In the far distance a farmer having finished his work in
one field goes toward another, a clumsy-looking hoelike implement
over his shoulder.

Toward the center of the town, that is, in the direction of the trading *buraku*, the activity and motion increase. Children appear in

---

[1]In this chapter I have followed somewhat the description of physical arrangements
and social organization of the Japanese rural village as given by the late John Embree
in his *Suye Mura*. I found, through observation of a considerable number of Japanese
villages, that Embree's conclusions about the single village, Suye Mura, were in fact
generally true of all Japan.

growing numbers as one approaches the business and administrative center. The youngsters are ever present, quietly agile but insatiably curious. Spots of color, notably lacking in the drab working clothes of the farm people, begin to enliven the scene. A vivid woman's kimono, a row of brightly colored bottles on a cake seller's counters, gilt and scarlet letters of some shopkeeper's advertisement catch the eye. Bicycle bells warn pedestrians. The ice cream peddler, the *icu creamu* man, with his blue box mounted behind him on a cycle makes his interminable round of brief trips between customers. The occasional "moo" of an ancient auto horn warns of the approach of a decrepit charcoal-powered vehicle, while a high-pitched screaming noise is the radio in a nearby store reporting the news from Tokyo. But all the while, motion and activity have picked up in intensity and volume. There are more people with more things to do and this makes for a sort of perpetual-motion kaleidoscope very different from one's idea of bucolic solitude. Perhaps it is the lack of automobiles and the throngs of pedestrians performing as conveyers and cargo carriers that help create the picture of motion and eternal busyness and impart a sense of drive and struggle.

The uniqueness of the village which, on its diminutive scale, almost creates the illusion of a Hollywood set, is not found in a single feature but in a total impression. Most Japanese houses are unpainted, so the prevailing tone is black or blackish grey. Ordinarily this monotony of color would be unattractive, yet there is something about the pitch of the roofs and the succession of horizontal roof peaks that gives a sense of lightness. This impression is heightened by the instinctive artistry with which trees and shrubs have been placed and trained. Attention, caught by the graceful curve of a spray of bamboo, the brightness of a single branch of flowering plum, a towering cryptomeria, or a carefully tended cypress hedge, is thus transferred from the drab unpainted effect of the buildings to the charm of their lines. True, there are ugly features of dirt and the evil smell of night-soil pits and overstrong fish, but they are counteracted somewhat by the delightful tiny roadside *Inari* shrines with bright red *torii* (arches in the Japanese fashion) which guard them. Bleak school grounds and buildings contrast with the cool shade of a small cryptomeria grove which perhaps shelters a Buddhist temple with its lovely tended precincts and carefully laid pathways. A small, roofed enclosure is a pleasant feature of most *buraku*. Here the children play their eternal quiet games watched by an old stone *Jizo*, to us an old upright stone, to them a person and a guardian.

Social Structure of the Village

Now that we have our stage we can distinguish among the people who move upon it. The largest group of villagers are, of course, the farmers. A much smaller group of specialists, carpenters, stone masons, cake makers, barbers, and, recently, hairdressers, provide

essential services. Often one or another of these specialists is lacking. Some villages have to depend on the occasional visits of specialists from another village, or perhaps a request is sent for a special
trip. Frequently these technicians are themselves part-time farmers.
Then there are the tradesmen, very small storekeepers who sell soybean cakes, some kinds of groceries, soy sauce, tinned fish, and soda
pop. A popular trader-specialist is the *tofu* (bean curd) maker, for
this ingredient used in making several kinds of highly prized dishes
is very popular with the housewives.

All these specialists and traders are no more than the social equals
of the farmers. Generally speaking, the farmer, if he owns land, is
their superior. The village officials, however, are definitely aristo-
crats; at least they are officially supposed to be, although some of
them lose face by appearing consciously "stuck-up." There is the
mayor or village headman who is an elected official. Sometimes there
is an assistant headman. Serving in the village office are one and
often two clerks. They are very useful, keeping track of all sorts of
vital records and statistics. In this office are maintained the permanent records of births, deaths, marriages, adoptions, as well as details
of land ownership and taxes. Here, too, is maintained a detailed account of the life of each individual in the village, commencing with his
birth and closing with his death. This is part of his family's docket in
which are similarly recorded all vital statistics of his entire family,
of his father, and perhaps of his father's father.

The roster of officials also includes school teachers who are appointed by the prefectural authorities. These teachers are not natives
of the village and do not reside in it permanently since they are subject to transfer from time to time. The same is true of the policeman
— 'Mr. Walking Around" — and the agricultural agent, although the
latter is not standard equipment and is not present in every village.
Then there is the dignified black-uniformed station master with his
large silver watch and scarlet cap band who stands so stiffly to attention when the train obediently departs in response to the blast on his
whistle.

But it is the unofficial rather than the official leaders who really
determine the village policies, guiding affairs through the invisible
controls of traditional unwritten authority. First, there are the family
heads of the *buraku*. Each person in the village is an official member
of some family either by blood or by adoption. Each family has an
official head whose authority is recognized by all the members on the
death of the father. As the juniors marry, they are sometimes established as branch families, so that an extended family which includes
branch families of junior members can get to be a fairly sizeable
affair in the course of a couple of generations. Heads of these groups
are important and venerated men carrying considerable weight in
buraku affairs.

Village headmen used to be elected by discussion among *buraku*
family heads. In addition to family headship, wealth also commands

respect and larger landholders outweigh smaller owners while both are superior to the tenant who doesn't count for much in *buraku* affairs. Younger people and women generally count for very little too, and usually have little authority. Older women, however, frequently come to have considerable authority within the family, particularly over the wives of their sons and grandsons.

Each *buraku* has several semi-official heads; all older men. Since these individuals carry full endorsements of the *buraku*, they are real leaders. There is the *buraku* leader himself, the *ku-cho*, regarded as a deputy of the village office. Actually, he is a deputy village headman. Then there are the leaders of the several *ku* cooperative organizations or *Kumiai* which handle *ku* economic and social affairs, such as rebuilding damaged bridges, maintaining roads, and cleaning irrigation ditches. In times of disaster these organizations are called on for a variety of chores and special tasks.

Buddhist and Shinto priests automatically carry weight in village and *buraku*. However, these clerics are neither celibate nor particularly sacrosanct. Sometimes they serve dual roles as part-time farmers or as clerks in village offices. At least in one case a priest was also village headman.

So now we have the stage and the dramatis personae of the Japanese village: fields, houses, roads, forests, farmers, village specialists, officials, and social leaders.

The Village as a Social and Economic Unit

But the force which sets this ensemble in motion is an urgent pressure for agricultural production: for food. Like the mainspring of a watch, recurrent pulsations of seed time and harvest, of planting and of cultivation, of preparation and of execution fundamentally determine the goings and comings, the waking and the sleeping; the days of activity, the days of ease, times of exertion, and times of repose. All real problems of the village are those of cultivators and all affairs of the village but reflect collective problems of cultivators. Is the rice seed ready? Will there be enough fertilizer? Will there be sufficient water for the paddy fields? Will the coming storm harm a ready harvest? These anxieties and others like them are the basic village concerns. All else awaits their answer. All thoughts, all questions, and all sense of well-being turn to the focal center of all interests – the cultivated land.

Out of this close relationship to land with its mysterious relation to germination and its real relation to the support of life, comes an intense attachment to it. Families and family members cling to ancestral plots in the face of all hazards. Sale of this land, even at considerable advantage, would, in most instances, not be considered at all. Even though a tract is disadvantageously located it would be an exceptional farmer who would think of exchanging it for a better located tract. Men fear lest they have no male offspring to inherit their family's land.

"If I have no son, then will I adopt one so that my fields will be cultivated in my family and my ancestors' graves and my own will be tended in honor for ever." No sorrow save the loss of an eldest son is as bitter as loss of land and no shame is like the shame of stepping down from ownership of land to tenant status. "For as I have land, so I am respected and live in honor and the more land, the greater the honor. From the heights of land ownership and the security of its production I gaze on lesser men, smaller landowners, unfortunate tenants. Even the headman, the priest, the schoolteacher are not more than my equals and — according to the code — we, they and I, acknowledge it."

Yet personal ambition and individual yearnings are subject to a severe social discipline in the Japanese village. Confucianism and Buddhism, received long ago from China, have combined with native Shinto beliefs to emphasize worship of the past, respect for tradition, and peaceful relations with one's community. One's niche in the village is a fixed point in the great facade of time and within the close-knit texture of the village one's movements are strictly limited. One's place in the social structure is not readily changeable. Indeed, the principal object of conduct is to preserve that place and hand it on with all its implied obligations and privileges to an eldest son. Now this position depends to a considerable degree on the opinion of neighbors who are all similarly conditioned. This opinion in turn is derived from a sum total of innumerable contacts with people of the *buraku* through the days of a man's lifetime. These contacts, in addition to a myriad of day-to-day relations include all the important events of existence — birth, schooling, marriage, death, as well as all business arrangements and all social contacts. Each of these contacts involves personal face-to-face relations. One's demeanor and bearing each day of one's life are the object of interest and attention of every one else.

It is little wonder that the Japanese are credited with a notable lack of facial expression. With so much at stake, so many ways in which one's secret thoughts could be disclosed, and so many acute observers, an inscrutable bearing would seem to be an essential requirement for any kind of comfortable living. In such a goldfish bowl existence, one cannot afford even the trivial expression of passing moods. One's daily changes of feeling and emotion are matters to be closely guarded lest misinterpretation and gossip follow.

The tight organization in which villagers are bound together permits literally no escape except to leave the village and seek a new life in the metropolitan area or in another village. But it is extremely difficult to make one's way in a new village since a newcomer faces a formidable adjustment in fashioning another place in the established configuration. For the villager there is, then, for all practical purposes no such thing as pulling up stakes and getting a new start. Thus a reasonably comfortable and secure existence for the individual is vitally dependent on avoiding conflicts, on cooperation, and on explicit conformity to accepted tradition and beliefs. In this framework of values there is practically no place for individualism. Confirmed individualists usually end by leaving the village and becoming a part of the metropolitan industrial labor force.

In order to maintain appearances, paying due respect to all village requirements, tortuous arrangements are sometimes necessary to avoid embarrassment. One selects a go-between to arrange a desirable marriage for one's son, so that in event of a refusal no embarrassment may disturb the smooth relations between families. One borrows money in secret so that one's economic difficulties may be hidden. The lender extracts his usurious rates stealthily so that the village makes no scandal of his greed. Landlords exert pressure on tenants to extort unfair rentals and both sides observe the code of secrecy.

One of the necessary conventions to this tight pattern of social discipline is acceptance of such secret behavior as proper, so long as the effort of concealment is made. In Japanese dramas, figures dressed in black are, by convention, invisible as they move scenery about in full view of the audience. Thus an embarrassing situation is simply not seen, provided a reasonable effort at concealment has been made. Everyone pretends complete ignorance of the situation.

There is a good side to all this emphasis on conformity and co-operation. Many undertakings possible through *buraku* cooperation are unattainable through individual effort and means. A man can give a party by borrowing utensils from the neighbors. He can get a new house built with *buraku* help by making arrangements with the village carpenter and the *buraku* authorities. An essential part of such an undertaking is the feast and drinking party marking the work's completion which he offers to his helpers. Indispensable help will be given a cultivator in transplanting the tender rice seedling in the spring and later in harvesting the crop. A villager and his family will enjoy many festivals at their neighbors' expense. These are only a few of the activities in which he will share and in which he will receive help.

But each of these occasions is based on the principle of reciprocity and the recipient must in his turn provide measure for measure. He will be called on to help at a neighbor's house-raising or with his neighbor's rice planting as well as at funeral ceremonies and festivities. At each party, as a guest, he brings a gift which is supposed to be precisely the equivalent value of a present which, as a host, he received on a previous occasion. All births, marriages, deaths, house-raisings, irrigation ditch cleanings, rice plantings are times of community activity. And each occasion is based on a fairly rigid unwritten code of approximate reciprocity. Failure to carry out these obligations not only as to time and amount but appropriately, with due recognition of the ceremonial manner prescribed for each occasion, amounts to non-cooperation in greater or less degree.

Such an omission is an extremely serious matter striking at

Neighbors help each other with the farm work, Gumma prefecture. (Courtesy, Dr. Hisayoshi Takeda.)

community survival. The group cannot exist except as a cooperative organism in which individuals play their parts according to established rules. Japanese villages make possible individual existence, and individuals, each acting in a predictable manner, according to an age-old code, sustain the village. Non-cooperation, or rather failure to contribute to community survival, is punished by a withdrawal from the offender's household of cooperation by the entire community. Ultimately this is equivalent to expulsion from the village.

Of course the ultimate sanction of total non-cooperation is not invoked all at once. Mild offenses are met with mild reprisals. One discovers if one fails to return gift for gift that one receives fewer and less desirable gifts. Should a man fail to show up when his turn comes to help a neighbor at planting time, he is likely to have difficulty in getting assistance for his own planting. Probably nothing would be said to the delinquent. The matter would never be allowed to reach the dimensions of an overt planned retaliation, nor would it ever be discussed except by oblique reference.

Thus everyone involved is saved embarrassment. Should the offender reform at this point, there is no record that anything has happened. Should he continue to deviate, still stronger sanctions might be invoked. Perhaps these sanctions might go so far as to conflict with official directives. For example, the delinquent might not get his full ration of government fertilizer from the village distributing center. Yet an official investigation of a complaint by the offending non-cooperator couldn't get very far for there would be nothing to go on. If pushed with sufficient vigor, it might be admitted, by the *buraku* officials, that a mistake had been made; but in general, the investigators would find no evidence of intent. There would be no conversations to relate, no threats to repeat, no gossip to remember.

Again, village taxes or imposts, based on informal judgments influenced by community sentiment, can be jockeyed to the disadvantage of a particular individual. Such a leverage would probably escape detection even in the event of an outcry. It might be possible that each individual case would be officially adjusted after a wrangle with constituted officials, but the recalcitrant would soon come to know that similar sanctions would be repeated as opportunity was presented. Moreover, he would not suffer alone. His whole family would feel the impact of community disfavor. His wife in her daily relations with the women of the community, his children at school and on the playground, would be helpless victims of a variety of humiliations and deprivations. Thus the community would assert its supremacy over the individual.

In many respects Western observers would find it difficult to quarrel with the basic economic aspects and ethical significance of this discipline. But on the negative side are implications of a tyranny, by a hierarchy of authority, freezing the individual into a caste system which he has been unable to challenge. Village cooperation involves acceptance of prerogatives of social rank and of the disabilities

attendant on inferiority. Recourse against injustice arising from
exercise of customary privilege of rank is not easily available, for
action by an inferior against a superior challenges the established
order. Such acts are viewed as lèse-majesté. The reaction appears
to be that such challenges threaten the security of all villagers.

The "Bright Village"

Sometimes the learned men in Tokyo, government specialist in
agrarian affairs, endow villages with specific personality traits,
speaking of an "honest village," "dirty villages," or "ignorant villages." Once, a few years ago, at a village meeting in Saitama prefecture, an Agricultural Ministry official attempted to outline for the
villagers a new national agricultural program in a question and answer session. After a baffling two-hour debate with the inhabitants
he said, "Come, let us find another village to talk with, *this village
is very stupid.*"

So ideals for improvement in agrarian affairs are often summed
up by Japanese in the term, "the bright village." "Bright villages"
are referred to as the goal of agrarian reform by Japanese agricultural economists, journalists, and bureaucrats. Sometimes specific
villages are designated as "bright" by officials who have visited them.
So the term has content and can be analyzed. To Westerners the use-
fulness of this term lies in the insight it gives into Japanese thinking.
Its meaning may be in contrast to our own concepts of desirable social
objectives expressed as "the free spirit," "the prosperous air,"
"community well-being," terms in which we might record our impres-
sions of an American community. One is convinced, however, that
while some of our terms are not incompatible with the "bright village,"
they certainly are not equivalent to the Japanese term.

By dint of much questioning and the comparison of different usages
one can get at the meaning through a consideration of what life in a
"bright village" might be like. Its chief feature would be a sort of
general peacefulness. Everyone would have sufficient prosperity to
be comfortable but would not, by his state, create envy among his
equals nor outrage his superiors by ostentation. Harmonious living
would characterize such a community, implying proper observation
of status and of individual movement within accepted spheres of behavior. Sound and motion would be muted. Life's scenes would appear
through the golden haze of a summer afternoon. Harsh noises, loud
voices, all discord would be absent. There would be color, life, ani-
mation, but, one gathers, in a somewhat stately tempo. Each individual would receive his due within the confines of his recognized place
in the scheme of things. From the whole community would emanate,
in a sedate and disciplined fashion, a gentle glow of serene happiness.
Such a condition, one feels, would be the *brightness* of the "bright
village."

It is clear that this concept is an oriental ideal of quietism, possibly

Confucian or Buddhist in origin. Basically it cherishes neither individual equality nor justice. Rather it idealizes communal peace and calm as the central objective of agrarian social arrangement. In such a context one conceives that personal justice would always be subordinate to community harmony. Desirable social and moral goals more or less universally accepted among Japanese would tend to inhibit recognition and correction of inequities within the village and of agrarian disabilities generally. Reform of these transgressions would shock and displace age-old relations, transforming the essential nature of the village itself while causing great insecurity to the villagers. A critical examination of the Japanese agrarian economy and the fundamental cleavages within the village reveals the "bright village" as an utterly impossible utopian myth and reform an unavoidable necessity.

Chapter 3

THE HISTORY OF THE JAPANESE PEASANTRY
AND ITS SIGNIFICANCE

THROUGHOUT the long centuries of Japanese history the peasants and their production have been the foundation on which were erected the structure of empire. These toiling men and women have been the silent nonvoting junior partners of the schemes of politicians and the dreams of military rulers for over twelve hundred years.

At about the same time that Charlemagne strove to reconstruct western Europe from the massive ruins of the Roman Empire, ambitious and somewhat bumptious Japanese leaders were endeavoring to construct a new kingdom out of a welter of warring tribes. Their model was China of the T'ang Dynasty. The magnificence, power, and dignity of the brilliant court of Cathay dazzled and fascinated the rustic lords of Nippon. Buddhist scholars were ardently entreated to visit the islands and preach their doctrines. Chinese art was eagerly studied and assiduously copied as were Chinese doctrines of government control.

Centralized Imperial Control

By the end of the eighth century the island rulers had constructed a central government which had some of the appearance but little of the spirit of its Chinese model. Whether they had foreseen it or not, these early political scientists soon found that in one respect the panoply of princely power was inseparable from a numerous bureaucracy who all possessed the common human need to consume food regularly. Courtiers, entertainers, judges, priests, poets, and soldiers alike could be maintained only if food in adequate amounts were continuously available. Inevitably, then, it was discovered that a government could govern significantly only after it had secured a food supply adequate to support itself. Thus, almost at the inception of organized central government in Japan, the land and the peasant stood forth as indispensable prerequisites of power. Thenceforth for more than twelve hundred years the farmer played the title role in the drama of Japanese history. At no time, of course, was he consulted in the making of momentous decisions of state policy which so closely affected him. Had he ventured an opinion, immediate death in a most unpleasant form would probably have been his lot.

Japanese kings early adopted a Chinese doctrine with regard to
land: "Under the heavens there is no land which is not the king's land;
among the holders of land there is none who is not the king's vassal."

Despite this all-embracing principle it took considerable time to
establish even an imperfect imperial control of agriculture. Efforts
to achieve it are reflected in several laws and edicts. In 645 A.D.,
the Reform of Taikwa was promulgated. This statute established
principles of land tenure, tax collection, accounting and statistical
procedures. Although larger land holdings of some families were
confirmed, the principal objective of the order was to insure the imperial household a substantial share of agricultural production. Land
was allotted to farm families in proportion to the size of the household. These holdings, called *ku-bunden*, "mouth share fields," were
revised every six years. This arrangement obviously implied a considerable bureaucratic apparatus of census taking and of account
keeping.

Comprehensive as this scheme was, it contained several weaknesses which eventually destroyed it. First, it had to be administered.
This placed considerable power in the hands of regional officials who
lacked Chinese traditions of altruism in government service and of
careful training for the administration of government. Consequently,
these administrators who were responsible for collecting the imperial
share of the rice crop to the imperial granaries soon found excuses
for delaying the deliveries. Now, in a simple economy such delays
amounted to a covert diversion of power, since power accompanied
physical possession of rice.

Second, and in the long run more significant, was the practice of
exempting certain lands from imperial control. Perhaps this usage
was an incident of the bargain by which lords were brought to accept
establishment of the new edict. In any case, it had the unfortunate
effect at the outset of creating two classes of land, lands under imperial control and lands exempt from imperial control. Power, then,
almost from the start was not concentrated in the hands of the ruler
but tended to be split three ways among rice-collection officials, the
ruler, and the holders of exempt lands. On the exempt lands, distribution of the produce was determined by the owner, making him in
effect a petty ruler.

With the development of the imperial court in scope, complexity,
and glamour, its needs for food expanded. As the needs of the Court
grew, so did the power of all those who controlled rice, and a considerable amount of power came to be controlled by hereditary chieftains.
To explain the rise of the hereditary system, one must recall that the
Japanese in establishing the much admired achievements of China in
the fields of religion, art, and government, took only the outward form.
They failed to capture the rich intellectual heritage and the essentially
democratic ethical spirit of the Chinese culture. They did not recognize, as China had, the need for a state service based on merit and
administered by an aristocracy of mental ability. Instead, they

substituted hereditary position and family. The state government structure of early Japan as set forth in the Code of Taiho (circa 700 A.D.), which was in large part copied directly from the Chinese, set up a hierarchy of state workers, ministers, and other functionaries in a rigid hereditary framework.

While all these plans and counterplans were in the making we can imagine that the farmers continued the ceaseless round of their occupation. Servants of the Emperor took a considerable portion of each farmer's output — so much for the labor tax which could be paid in kind, so much for the land tax, and so much from any production other than rice. If these burdens became too unbearable, perhaps the farmer and his family stealthily deserted their tiny plot and resettled on the exempt land of some powerful lord or on that of a temple. If he remained on the *ku-bunden* land, he was allotted about half an acre for each male in the family and about a third of an acre for each female in the family, or about two acres for a family of five people. Of course, there was no guarantee that he would permanently improve his lot by running off to the exempt land, but there might be an immediate gain. For, after all, land without producers is of no value, so often the owners of exempt land were anxious to obtain more workers and sometimes were willing to grant concessions to new settlers. But there were wars to be fought too and in these the farmer was liable to service. If he survived, sometimes he was lucky enough to gain status as a freeholder, still under the lord's protection.

The Decentralized Feudal State

Meanwhile in Nara and later in Heian and Kyoto, life in the imperial court became more complex, more polished, more educated, and more cultured. But the inherent weakness of the position of the Emperor and the waxing power of the powerful clans daily brought closer the seizure of active control by the great lords and the relegation of imperial rule to the status of a gilded symbolism. Power once seized by these clans from weaker clans in the long periods of internecine strife became fixed by inheritance. Finally there emerged three great feudal clans, the Taira, the Minamoto, and the Fujiwara. The families of these clans, in one way or another, as imperial regents, as court advisors, or as military rulers, dominated Japanese political history to the middle of the nineteenth century. The government was transformed from a central establishment, based on the authority of imperial power at Kyoto, to control from the headquarters of a series of semifeudal military lords representing one branch or another of the three clans.

The central factor in the rise of these clans and in their maintenance of power was the ability to control agricultural production, principally rice. As the result of that resource they welded together a substantial and permanent military establishment. Power was fundamentally a function of rice production. Government became essentially the art of dividing the harvest among producers, feudal functionaries, lords of the land, military leaders, and clan families in such a way as to maintain a balance of power, a maximum of loyalty, and a minimum of independence. Above all, this procedure meant a manipulation of the peasants who produced the rice. It was therefore necessary to control every aspect of their lives throughout the entire period.

This objective was accomplished through the institutions of religion, of family life, and of the community and by the organization of the feudal estate. One of the principal elements of this system was a compulsory subdivision of rural villages into groups of five families. Members of these *gonin kumiai* were mutually responsible for maintenance of law and order within the group and for taxes of any defaulting members. Other aspects of the system were the feudal institutions of *benefice* and *commendation*. By these, the inferior individual obtained the protection of the feudal superior in return for loyalty and servitude.

Thus, each private domain or *shoen* consisted of loosely grouped small units of individual cultivation. Actually, the peasant cultivator of each parcel enjoyed only a vague cultivation right and the questionable security of a sadly deficient sustenance. Yet this arrangement was sufficient to create a vivid and enduring sense of proprietorship which he cherished deeply. In addition to his cultivation rights the peasant had other rights *(shiki)* in respect to irrigation, fishing, woodcutting, and taking of game. These privileges with cultivation rights fitted into a much broader pattern of *shiki* which in effect covered the whole of feudal society. But these rights in turn were granted by nonproducers who retained always the privilege of receiving specified amounts of the rice crop. Thus all aspects of feudal life were based on agricultural production; it was the very heart of the feudal system. In the roster of feudal lords who ruled all or parts of Japan for seven centuries it was only those who recognized the vital significance of the peasant who ruled wisely.

Repression Under Tokugawa Rule

After nearly five hundred years of pulling and hauling for power among the three great clans, the Japanese settled down to nearly two and a half centuries of relatively peaceful centralized rule under the Tokugawa family. During this period of *shogun* rule the nation was completely cloistered. Shut off from any foreign intercourse whatever, the country moved in the narrow orbit of strict feudal controls. The imperial capital remained at Kyoto but the seat of government was at Edo (Tokyo).

The constant objective of the Tokugawa rule was a completely static society. Consequently, they regarded the affairs of the farm people with minute attention and exercised a detailed control of their lives. The virtues inculcated were those which exalted the past. Loyalty to one's ancestors and feudal superiors was a supreme obligation and to this objective the Shinto religion was a powerfully effective instrument. In addition quietistic Buddhist and Confucian principles emphasized peace in the village and acceptance of one's lot. As a matter of plain fact, it was to everyone's advantage, except the farmer's, to devise a whole system of morals to justify to themselves and to the farmers the extraction of an ever increasing portion of his production.

Farmers, under the Tokugawas, were given to understand that, although important members of society, yet they were incapable of handling ordinary affairs of business. "Agriculture is the mainstay of the state," a popular saying of these times, stated only a principle of agrarian feudal policy, not a principle of respect for farmers. In 1649, farmers were officially described as possessing neither prudence nor wisdom. Efforts were made to separate peasants from other groups, particularly from knowledge of the pleasures and luxuries of city life. One sage wrote: "Farmers should by no means imitate the mode of living of townspeople." The advice of another wise man was that "farmers should not wed their children to those of townspeople." Ignorance of their own affairs and how these stood in relation to other affairs was considered a sound way for farmers to achieve happiness. Such ignorance was rated a virtue according to an economic text of that time which held that "it is a good farmer who does not know the prices of cereals." One can only comment that if such a precept were followed in our time, it would certainly have left few domestic topics with which to occupy our statesmen!

Yet all this attention to the farm problem by the wise men of the Tokugawa era seems to indicate that some sort of a problem existed. Indeed one did exist. For, as the Tokugawa regime waxed in power, it accumulated an increasingly large nonproductive following with a corresponding appetite for farm produce. This desire could only be satisfied by shoving forward another notch or several notches the demands on farmers. Nor could these oppressive lords stay the steady unseen pressure and interplay of economic forces of whose very existence they were ignorant. Yet these trends gradually offset and undermined the crude administrative techniques of feudalism and ended by unraveling completely that tissue of power.

Breakdown of Tokugawa Control

For quite a while, however, things seemed to move in a more or less controlled manner. True, there was some dissatisfaction which from time to time required stern repression. But these disturbances were probably dismissed as mere incidents in an otherwise successful and even glorious regime. Perhaps in the sunset of a political and economic system it seems to its beneficiaries that its glory sheds its brightest beam.

The gradual deterioration of Tokugawa power had progressed sufficiently by 1800 so that the final period to its downfall in 1868 was a continual series of crises. These were met by measures which were

mostly oppressive and often cruel. Two dynamic factors seem to
have been principally responsible for this situation. One was the
gradual spread of money as a means of exchange to replace the older
methods of barter and goods exchange; the other, in part a result of
the first, was the gradual development of an independent rice market
which evaded the controls of government. The root of evil in the para-
dise of the latter Tokugawa days was the ability of those who controlled
rice to borrow money in advance of the harvest from traders in the
growing market centers of the Osaka district. Osaka grew to be the
central rice market. Markets historically are the carriers of revolution, more deadly to autocratic government in their silent working than
all the intellectual ideology of revolution or the armed might of outright hostility.

As we have seen, the ability to control production and distribution
of food was the key to control of feudal Japan. But the luxury-loving
lords of that time failed to comprehend the havoc wrought in that system by the mortgage of a rice crop to an Osaka dealer. All they sought
was money to erect a new castle or to provide a cherished concubine
with lovely surroundings and appropriate entertainment. Moreover,
the significance of the intricacies of trade appears to have escaped
the understanding of the authorities. What happened when one dealer
sold his mortgage to another, and he to still another and so on, until a
whole system of transactions was woven like a silken net that entangled
the whole economic structure seems to have been a baffling mystery.
Finally it was too late and the feudal noblemen awoke to find that it
was the despised merchants, the *Chonin,* and not they, who controlled
the rice of Japan.

As the economy of money and markets developed, farm costs increased and the relative standard of living of the peasants declined.
Their feudal superiors caught in the same trap sought escape by increasing their demands for rice production. So the whip descended on
the wracked backs of the peasantry, and with the increasing tempo of
change the whip descended more heavily and frequently. This suffering was met by efforts to escape it. The increasing attractiveness of
city life served as a beacon drawing to its light many seeking release
from the rigors of rural life. So the cities grew. Tokyo grew to
metropolitan size largely by the influx of these fugitives from the rice
paddies. This increase in metropolitan population with its increasing
economic demands served to intensify the speed of the underlying
transformation. Farmers who remained on the farms were called
upon for extra production. They sought to decrease their own consumption by reducing the size of their families through the dreadful
institution of infanticide – killing their infant offspring.

This custom, called *Mabiki* (thinning) was widespread throughout
Japan in the latter part of the eighteenth and first part of the nineteenth centuries. The practice of infanticide and abortion significantly
affected the size of the rural population in northeastern Japan. In
Kyushu families customarily murdered two out of five children.

Farmers of Tosa province reared only three children. In other districts only male children were spared and in Hyuga province only the eldest male child survived. Half-grown or adolescent children kidnapped in Osaka and Kyoto were sold to farmers who thus obtained an additional worker without the expense of child rearing.

Under these conditions land went out of production. Production fell off. General misery increased. However, with the weakening of the feudal bonds which inevitably occurred, it became possible along with trading in rice to trade also in land. Now, feudalism implies among other things that land transfers are the sole prerogative of the fief holder. The cultivator and the land are inseparable. Hence, trading land by cultivators was a sure sign of the decay of feudalism and of the emergence of a free economy. Land was sold to those able to buy it, namely, to rich people. But not to the feudal lords since nominally they already owned the land. More practically they were a debtor class without the means of purchase. So a new class of richer landowners was created by this process. A large part of the transactions resulted from debt with the debtor remaining on the land as a tenant of the new owner in the case of foreclosure. The new owners were at first careful to conciliate the titular feudal lords whose domain they had entered as a nonfeudal entrepreneur.

Thus, out of flight from the land, infanticide, and trading in land could be glimpsed beneath the fraying garments of feudal institutions the new pattern of land tenure which was later to characterize the agrarian system of modern Japan. But this new pattern, developing out of the older system of relations, never freed itself of many of the qualities of its matrix. Particularly in economic and social relations, modern agrarian Japan carried over and maintained significant aspects of feudalism. In contrast to life in the great metropolitan areas of Tokyo, Yokohama, Osaka, Kobe, and Nagasaki, the ways of Oharame and the thousands of other rural villages remained as reservoirs of ancient traditions and of static institutions. The cherished virtues were stubborn resistance to change and insistence on conduct conforming to the old stern code of obedience and loyalty.

One of the specific virtues of feudalism in contrast to the anarchy of the time preceding it was the protection of the vassal under the feudal lord. In turn the vassal served his lord. The servitude was often cruel but there was also the direct obligation of the lord, which was just as compelling, to protect his people. Thus the peasant had a compulsion to serve his superiors despite hardship. Revolt against a superior, signifying a rejection of obligations, implied grave moral responsibility. Such sanctions were not as clear in the newer tenant-landlord relations of the latter Tokugawa period.

In that confused and uncertain interlude, the peasants were still held fast in a feudal framework. They nominally owed all the original loyalties of former times to a feudal superior, and in addition to these obligations, many of them became enmeshed in economic responsibilities to nonfeudal landlords with whom they had entered into separate business arrangements outside the feudal system. But a cultivator's right to feudal protection from oppression by the new landowners was at best shadowy. This was the inevitable result of economic bargains outside the area of feudal obligation and in many instances in direct violation of feudal law. Thus the new landlords could and did squeeze their tenants. Tenants, on the other hand, were almost helpless in the grip of this manifestation of the cash economy. The new landlord class was not slow to take advantage of the moral dilemma of the new tenant group. Quickly, they converted economic to social superiority by various means such as intermarriage with impoverished feudal lords or by the outright purchase of entry into the feudal family via the prevalent custom of adoption. Thus the emerging tenant class found itself still bound by feudal obligations, although receiving less and less of the feudal benefits. Yet at the same time, the tenants became social inferiors to a new class of economic overlords who thus cloaked themselves, albeit somewhat spuriously, with the mantle of feudal sovereignty.

One method of expression remained to these new tenants. It appeared to them that no feudal sanctions clearly forbade a revolt against the authority of the parvenu landlord group. Soon peasant revolts reverberated throughout Japan, lasting throughout the closing periods of the feudal era. Indeed, unbearable conditions of life made such peasant outbreaks almost the only alternative to their extinction. If farmers cultivated efficiently, rent was raised to confiscate the increased harvest. If yields were low, the landlord's take reduced the tenant to starvation. The situation in the last century of feudalism was further complicated by widespread and prolonged crop failures accompanied by famine and plague.

Peasants tried several methods of escaping from these insuperable difficulties. At about the time of the American Revolution, tenant-landowner disputes took the form of a strike. Tenants over a wide area of Japan offered to give up cultivation and to return their land to the lord. Of course landlords learned to practice effective counter-stratagems. In a series of disturbances extending from 1843 to 1857, landlords met petitions for redress from their tenants with several measures designed to break tenant combinations, including universal blacklisting. A strange and peculiarly Japanese note was the frequent voluntary surrender, after an outbreak, of the peasant leaders, who were thereupon ceremoniously and horribly put to death. Apparently both sides regarded this sacrifice as a sort of ritual atonement for the loss of face suffered by the lord in whose domain the disturbance had occurred.

These skirmishes culminated in open conflict. Minor riots flared into widespread revolts which finally were intermingled with and obscured by the general uprising which ended the period. Thus peasant distress and the rebellion associated with it were partially responsible for the final downfall of feudalism and the emergence of the modern Japanese era in 1868. From another viewpoint it may be suggested

that the failure of the feudal rulers of Japan to solve the agrarian
problem revealed the need of a different system of government which
was enforced by popular demand.

The Peasantry and Imperial Expansionism

With the Meiji Restoration in 1868 the functional role of agriculture and of the peasants had a somewhat different significance. New
factors and considerations of government brought different agrarian
requirements and somewhat different kinds of pressure on the cultivators. Formerly, control of agriculture had been a central problem
of a government which sought to preserve a static, closed feudal system. Under Meiji, however, agrarian affairs became a feature in a
vast plan for creating an empire in the modern world.

The scope of Japan's development as an empire far exceeds the
dimensions of this book. Nevertheless, in order to explain the role of
rural Japan in this scheme, a consideration of the spirit and aspirations associated with empire will perhaps be illuminating. For neither
a description of the Japanese peasant nor the picturesqueness of the
Japanese rural scene serves as a base to comprehend the terrific
dynamic inherent in the post-Restoration program of imperial expan-
sionism.

It should be emphasized that rural simplicity, gentleness, and
pastoral placidity were not dominant characteristics of the new development. Yet many of these aspects coexisted with the new undertaking. Too often in the past, Westerners have been beguiled by the
lovely countryside of Japan and the charming ways of its rural people
to disregard or underestimate the grandeur of Japanese ambitions.
Yet it is patent that very profound considerations transcending the
agrarian scene were required to explain the startling material achievement of the Japanese in the last 80 years.

A review of these achievements reveals that savage ambition,
ceaseless energy, and a sustained driving pride must have been almost
indispensable requirements not only of a few leaders but of almost the
entire nation. An observer, engrossed in Japanese rural scenes and
with agrarian problems, who confronts for the first time the vast material evidences of empire must often revalue all his previous conclusions. Yet both are Japan. And each aspect must be examined with
the other clearly in mind. One must remember the Japanese farm
scene when gazing, today, at the formidable naval installations at
Yokusuka or the enormous ruins of the Nagoya aircraft plants. One
shudders at the almost incredible destruction wrought by American
B-29s in the vast intricate expanse of dry docks, submarine installations, and naval rifle works that were only part of the great secret
naval base at Kure. Standing in the midst of this wreckage of rusty
steel and blasted concrete the thought continually recurs, "How could
it have been done? How could all the wealth and labor that these
achievements represent have derived from the limited resources of
these four small islands?"

How was all this accomplished by a feudal agrarian people possessing in 1868 the minimum of knowledge of Western science, technology, and methods of thought? How could men who had an almost entirely nonscientific and even an alogical intellectual heritage master so quickly all the necessary science and technology of Europe and America? How did a nation thus intellectually equipped, with extremely slender natural resources create a vast industrial plant in less than 75 years?

We know that only 35 years after commencement of the modern era, Japan defeated Imperial Russia, using modern military equipment and strategy. Twenty-seven years later, in 1930, Japan had become one of the great textile manufacturing nations of the world. Moreover, she was an active participant in world trade in several other lines. Noguchi and other Japanese scholars and scientists had achieved world fame. In transportation, remarkable progress was evident. Japan has possessed for many years an admirable railroad system covering all four islands, and up to World War II her merchant fleet placed her among the principal modern deep-water trading nations. These are only some of the more outstanding achievements which by 1935, 67 years after the Meiji Restoration, entitled Japan to a leading place among the nations of the world.

The speed and scope of Japanese accomplishment contrast with limited resources both in technological background and in basic raw materials. Thus the development was a triumph of planning and determination. But neither effort would have been adequate without an underlying principle of authority which assured planners and rulers alike of a completely organized nation whose population and resources were capable of mobilization for the undertaking. In effect, this accomplishment meant integration of an entire population into a single grand labor force susceptible of complete domination by a directing authority. This was achieved by exploiting twin principles of religion and political solidarity – duty to spiritual doctrines of Shinto and adoration of an Emperor.

Initially this program was based on a domination of agricultural production, the only substantial resource of that day. Thus land and peasants were the cornerstones of imperial structure. The only other resources were timber, fisheries, and sites for later hydroelectric development. Except for low-grade coal, metals and other mineral resources were entirely inadequate. Also deficient for any industrial expansion were fats, oils, and fabric materials. Livestock and livestock products were very thinly distributed among the population. So the rulers of Japan at the beginning of the modern era, as they had done a thousand years earlier, placed on the shoulders of the farmer almost the entire burden of the plan for dominion. Farmers were limited by soil and climate almost entirely to a restricted production consisting of small grains, potatoes, and silkworms.

Chapter 4

THE PEASANTRY AND THE MODERN ERA

W E HAVE seen that in the latter Tokugawa days outworn feudal land tenure relations of vassal and feudal lord were being supplanted by a tenure system characterized by land ownership obtained through cash purchase. Tenancy was the result of a rent bargain whose terms were dictated by the owner. Now, under Meiji, remaining feudal land institutions were systematically replaced with modern fee simple ownership. By a series of statutes culminating in 1873 the new central government appraised and paid off the feudal right holders thus ending that system and creating one of universal private ownership.[1]

A principal objective of this move was to secure a regular and substantial source of revenue. Paid in cash, tax revenues from landowners served as a base for national credit. As a result of the new agrarian settlement, land could be bought, sold, or mortgaged at will by private citizens using money as a medium of exchange. Although the new Meiji statesman would perhaps have preferred to have had a system of owner-cultivators, this pattern did not develop because landowners found it much more profitable to rent their land to tenants.

Tenancy, a Characteristic of Japanese Agriculture

Thus, subsequent land tenure development took a completely different turn in Japan from that occurring in Europe with the appearance there of fee simple ownership. In the latter case the new ownership class found it more profitable to operate their own farms with their own capital and managerial ability. But the Japanese landowners in many instances were discouraged from such a course by high rentals which land-hungry farmers were willing to pay. Consequently, the principal effect of the Meiji Restoration on the land tenure of Japan was to project into the modern period the earlier tenant situation developed under the Tokugawas minus the feudal rights of lords. However, the new system still retained a feudal atmosphere with tenants relegated to an inferior social status. This situation laid a groundwork

---

[1] In this chapter I have amplified somewhat the discussion of the early Meiji period as originally published in my *Japanese Land Reform Program*. As indicated in that earlier publication, the source of the material included Mr. E. Herbert Norman's *Japan's Emergence as a Modern State*.

for the development of three principal agrarian classes which existed up to the close of World War II. It consisted of: (1) those who owned and cultivated land, (2) those who cultivated but did not own land, and (3) those who owned but did not cultivate. Among cultivators, then, there were owners and tenants; among owners there were landlords and cultivators.

But owner-cultivators, initially in the majority, suffered from want of cash, the chronic complaint of farmers everywhere under a cash economy. Let us consider the hypothetical case of Tanaka-san (the Japanese equivalent of Joe Doakes), a Japanese owner-cultivator of that period. Now Tanaka-san, or Joe Tanaka, toiled mightily on his two-acre farm. The price he received for this crop then, represented his entire annual cash income. This price resulted from trading on the central exchange at Osaka. High prices of course were the result of a short national harvest, so Tanaka-san sold a smaller harvest for a higher price per unit. If yields were abundant, prices were low, so Joe got smaller prices for a larger crop.

In any event, the Tanaka family received this cash all at one time in the fall of the year after the harvest. This cash lump sum had to suffice not only for all family living needs until the next harvest, but it had to cover costs of cultivation, fertilizer, seed, and payment of taxes as well. Joe had to pay for all these items out of the cash he received for his rice, but prices for these items were unrelated to prices for his product. Indeed it sometimes happened before the next harvest rolled around that he was buying rice for food at a price higher than that for which he had sold it. Unfamiliar with money and its ways, Tanaka-san was frequently unable to stretch the money which he received all at one time over the period till the next harvest.

Particularly was Tanaka-san unprepared to meet extremely heavy taxes which had to be paid in cash. So he borrowed. But, since borrowing in rural Japan is somewhat of a disgrace, he procured money in secret from a local private usurer by putting up the family farm as security. Soon after, Joe, unable to keep up with interest charges which were not infrequently as high as 30 per cent, found himself a tenant on his own family's farm.

There was no lease agreement, no contract as we understand the term. Rather, the tenant was the landlord's man, respectful to him as a superior, unquestioning of his demands, subservient to terms he set. In short, there was no contract because there was really no bargain; only utter need on the one hand and command of a basic resource on the other. There were only landlord requirements which the tenant must accept or leave off farming. In such circumstances rents were high and generally paid in kind. Poor Tanaka-san and many, many like him, now found himself free of some of his tax burden, but instead of facing the year's problems with the proceeds of 80 bushels of rice as formerly, he now had at most 40 bushels, since the other 40 bushels went as rent. Rents in kind varied in different rice paddy areas from 50 to 70 per cent.

Now all this was pretty hard on Tanaka-san, but from the point of
view of the empire-builders it worked rather well. The landlord
group became a source of government credit. They bought government bonds, thus providing money capital sorely needed by the
empire-builders. Joe Tanaka didn't know it, of course, but the crops
he grew were transformed into all sorts of things that he had never
dreamed of: factories, warships, submarine tunnels, like the one
under the straits of Shimonoseki. Yet Joe Tanaka, the little brown
rice grower, with his smiling wife and pretty babies, was the mainspring that made the whole thing move.

Between 1880 and 1890 the expropriation of small cultivators proceeded at a rapid pace; a wholesale social transition was under way.
By 1892, 24 years after Meiji, the process of taxes and usury had
worked to bring nearly 40 per cent of all Japanese farmers under the
yoke of tenancy. Farm tenancy thus emerged as a fixed characteristic
of Japanese agriculture, along with rice and night soil, a necessity
attendant on the journey of a people toward its destiny. The peasantry,
too, were a necessity of empire planning and the place allotted them
in the scheme of things required from them many duties and disabilities. Until recently, Japanese farmers have truly been forgotten men
in the search of a nation for material progress and modern ways. Yet
all the time farmers were the base on which the pyramid of imperial
plans rested.

True, the policy makers gave some thought to agriculture. Clever
scientists did an excellent job in developing strains of rice, well
adapted to the seasonal variations and island growing conditions.
Other crops were likewise improved. Careful analysis established
precise chemical fertilizer requirements. Attention was given to
agricultural research generally; institutions of agricultural learning
associated with Tokyo, Hokkaido, and Kyushu Imperial Universities
produced some very good agronomic and agricultural scientists. In
these and in many other ways attention was given to the technical
phases of agricultural production. But there appears to have been
tacit agreement among all in authority to leave rural life strictly
alone. Peasants were to remain much as they always had been, patient
producers of basic foodstuffs and begetters of loyal sons of the soil.

The set of duties, obligations, loyalties, and customs which constitute the social network of Japanese rural life combined to hold the
peasant in this thralldom of service. Intense love of the land which
his ancestors had cultivated immobilized him occupationally. Although
expropriated, yet he was able by the tenancy system to remain on the
land. Duty to his parents and ancestors forced him to continue in
established ways particularly in his relations to social superiors including his landlord. Duty to the Emperor implied unquestioned acceptance of all government decrees including tax measures. Pride or
sense of face forced him to deal secretly with usurers who shame-
lessly fleeced him. A pride in living within the old stern frugal code
of the samurai made him a sucker for all kinds of nationalist jingoism.

Rural folk were traditionally supporters of a militaristic order which fully exploited for its own ends the warrior's code with its trappings of force, self-sacrifice, and class distinction.

It would be unfair to imply that the material progress of this nation did not bring some gains to rural areas. For example, universal elementary education taught village children to read and write a little. Yet, in spite of limited material improvements, rural life retained much of the misery of feudalism. Particularly was this true for the millions of farm families who lived as tenants under that unfree and exploitive system.

Aspects of Farmer Resistance

Tenants, while not precisely a social class, nevertheless bore common economic and social burdens. However, except for payment of rent, smaller owners shared similar disabilities. Too, small owners always stood on the brink of tenancy and many had slipped part way over the brink as renters of part of the land they cultivated.

Immediately following World War I, Japanese tenants and small owners, already staggering under loads of debt, rent, and taxes, were still further burdened with adverse economics of that postwar era. When prices moved, they moved widely, and falling rice prices were sometimes accompanied by rising prices of other commodities.

But in this period a new spirit was abroad in the land. Perhaps for the first time, Japanese were made aware of the existence of doctrines and beliefs of personal freedom and of the possibility of society organized on democratic principles. Germany, whom Japan admired greatly and whose leadership and genius the Japanese had attempted to follow in education, science, and law, became a military enemy. Japan, allied with America, Britain, and France, partook, albeit somewhat remotely, of the democratic ideology and propaganda of her allies. Miscellaneous tag ends of these doctrines and beliefs eventually filtered through to rural areas. Perhaps for the first time, the idea of individual rights gained some color of respectability among Japanese. At least it could hardly be denied that Japan had participated in a major war on the side of those who held such ideals.

Unrest among the disadvantaged farm people followed. Expressions of dissatisfaction of the later Tokugawa era were mostly wild frenzies of despair. But in the third decade of the twentieth century, reaction to peasant distress began to express itself by political and economic organization. Tenant-landlord disputes, formerly little more than recorded arguments, increased in severity and scope. Often these agrarian wrangles had a collective social character involving in the same dispute considerable numbers of tenants and several landlords. Their political significance lay in their obvious challenge to traditional patterns of social status. In 1936, 6,804 of these controversies were recorded in all parts of the country. On the average, each dispute involved four landlords and twenty tenants.

Far more of a challenge to the existing order than tenant-landlord disputes, was the formation in 1922, by peasants, of a farmers' organization, The Japan Farmers Union *(Nihon Nomin Kumiai)*. One doubts if the simple men of the pygmy farms could have realized fully their temerity in taking this step. Yet it most certainly did bring them to official attention. In 1925, still unabashed, they formed a Farmer Labor Party whose official existence of about three hours was terminated by government order. Apparently the memory of this ill-fated venture into explicit political organization was a sufficient deterrent to further overt provocation in that direction, for in succeeding years, we find farm organizations concentrating almost exclusively on economic questions.

One can imagine the serious concern with which these events were viewed by Japanese elder statesmen. This powerful group, despite all the modern devices which it had introduced, nevertheless clung firmly to principles of autocracy and strict enforcement of a social caste system. The emergence of self-determining and spontaneously organized farm groups which sought no sponsorship and requested no permission from established authority must have seemed bad enough. Those keen enough perceived the implicit significance of such groups as a threat to established agrarian economic and social relations. In a wider sense, this challenge may have appeared to extend, not only to landlordism, but to state policy and the imperial program as well.

Needless to say, the way was not made easy for these pioneers of agrarian self-liberation. True, they were not overtly put out of business. Their existence received no express disapproval. Yet it must have been clear to their leaders, at least, that they were objects of disapproval. In various ways, the new farmers' unions were subjected to official pressure. Harassment of their leaders, in the form of occasional terms in jail, was one form of coercion. Another came from the acute consciousness of the members themselves that their actions contradicted basic ethical principles of obedience, acceptance of established social arrangements, etc. These forebodings were exploited by the authorities in many ways. But the movement, always under pressure, never overcoming its initial handicaps, survived to the end of the thirties. It almost completely disappeared in the war years. As an indicator of a trend towards resistance to economic injustice, its significance is far greater than either its achievements or the number of its members. As a catalytic agent for the initiation of national agricultural planning, the movement had perhaps its widest significance.

The Japanese government had urgent need to keep control of agrarian affairs in its hands. Consequently, the issue of agrarian reform, once raised as a goal for independent peasant organization, away from government, became of necessity a matter for government action. For if government wanted to continue full control of agriculture, it must assert its authority by providing an answer to basic peasant problems.

Nor was the government hierarchy slow to take action. A perfect

rash of proposals for agrarian reform broke out in the Diet. Others
were put forward by the Ministry of Agriculture and Forestry. A
measure enabling tenants to purchase land was enacted in 1922 and
revised in 1926. A Cooperative Societies Law enacted around the
turn of the century was refurbished. A Tenancy System Investigation
Commission was set up and made some sound, although vague, recommendations in 1926. The principal direction of these initial steps was
toward provision of cheap money on liberal repayment terms to permit peasants to regain ownership status. Other measures like the
Farm Tenant Conciliation Law of 1924 sought to soothe the disturbed
atmosphere of the village by providing machinery for arbitrating
tenant-landlord disputes.

Unfortunately, these initial measures were not very effective. The
government and its advisors sought the largest possible returns from
the fewest possible concessions. Then, of course, there was an opposition composed of traditionalists to whom any change in peasant
status was anathema. There were the landlords who for obvious reasons desired no change. Consequently, these measures were not forthright in their espousal of the peasants' cause. Any relief they offered
required lengthy complex processes, too often beyond the comprehension of a simple villager. Moreover, they all sought to preserve the
status quo. Hence, beyond their value as historical landmarks on the
way to the establishment of later reforms, they had little merit. A
measure for enabling tenants to become landowners, for example, did
not require landlords to sell their land and failed to control land
prices. Consequently, landlords refused to sell land at all or offered
it at prohibitive prices. Failure of the measure is indicated by a net
increase of 9,000 in the number of tenants between 1926 and 1936,
years of the law's most intensive application.

Militarism and the Farmer 1821897

By 1930 it must have been clear to everyone, and particularly village folk, that Japanese agriculture and Japanese farmers were in a
very bad way. Moreover, in the decade since World War I, shocking
discrepancies between pleasant myths of harmonious rural peace and
the actual deplorable situation had become widely known through parliamentary debate and public discussion. The genial feudal superior,
protecting his vassals in time of trouble, now appeared for the first
time to many Japanese as a parasite, living on the exertion of his
tenants, indifferent to their misery. In many cases, it turned out, the
landlord was an absentee owner, no longer having the slightest interest
in village affairs. While still obscure, the outline of the terrific usury
problem was beginning to become clear. Problems of rice prices
were causing a great deal of concern and various measures to stabilize
agricultural prices were under consideration as a result.

Then the world-wide economic collapse of 1929 brought all these
problems to a head. Rice prices collapsed and the entire rural economy

was reduced to chaos. At the same time all other segments of the economy were in turmoil. Elsewhere in the world this troublesome period served as the trigger to set off major political upheavals with strong militaristic overtones, and Japan was no exception. The Japanese military clique with its tradition of duty, loyalty, stern self-discipline, and allegiance to the old feudal code of the samurai was a natural political ally of the peasants. Both groups cherished the same cultural myths. It was easy to believe that Japan's trouble arose from the softness of modern ways and the general wickedness of metropolitan groups. Of course farmers were already jealous of these urban folk with their slick ways and the military despised them. Moreover, a majority of enlisted personnel, most non-commissioned officers, and many junior officers of the Japanese army, were of rural origins. So, quite frequently, the Japanese farm family was tied closely and personally to the military.

After a man joined the army, he was encouraged to maintain strong ties with his village. His officers occasionally wrote his parents or village officials reporting his progress in military training. More rarely, personal visits of army officers to the village were occasions for honoring parents of soldiers. On such occasions the whole gamut of feudal loyalties was stressed, ancestors, family, household gods, the emperor, and Great Japan — *Dai Nihon*, all were duly acknowledged and enthused over. No wonder then that simple peasantry embraced this relationship wholeheartedly, for in addition to its emotional stimulation, there were sound economic reasons for the alliance. A son in the army regularly sent home part of his tiny pay; also, he was army fed and clothed. These gains relieved straitened family budgets to that extent. So, to glory reflected from a son who served the emperor, there was added a net economic gain. Nor was this all; for the military politicians, speaking on public matters with a voice to be heeded, frequently took occasion to chide the business and commerical community, holding them responsible for the farmers' plight. This was sweet music to sorely pressed farmers.

Finally, military leaders interpreted their own dreams of empire and conquest to meet aspirations of farmers. Wide vistas of opportunity for settlement in new lands to be conquered would relieve pressure on the fields of the homeland. Great Japan would spread her imperial mantle over fields and farms of inferior peoples to benefit her own peasant emigrants under the protection of the Rising Sun banner.

A weird combination of Tolstoyan socialism, *Mein Kampf*, Marxism, and native Shinto beliefs served as the ideological nucleus around which militant, semicriminal secret societies were formed in several rural districts. These organizations seldom got into action, remaining enmeshed in a fantastic welter of plots and counterplots. Yet they did manage partly by intent, partly by accident, to murder a few moderate leaders. While such fanatical organizations and their deeds were unrepresentative of the peasant group as a whole, nevertheless in an extreme form they did, perhaps, express something of the spirit of the times. They certainly found a pattern in the direct action attitude of the military and its own deeds of violence.

But, in spite of the patently unstable nature of the farmer-military alignment, the military did set about to reform the agrarian situation. In fact, as a result of military sponsorship the agrarian reform movement after 1930 caught fire and received widespread enthusiastic support. The number of measures of agrarian reform put forward in the ensuing period probably exceeded the total of all such measures proposed since the beginning of the Meiji era. These included new measures and revisions of older ones for land purchase by tenants, protection of tenants against unfair losses, debt adjustment, formation of cooperatives, and regulation of prices for land and farm products.

Tanaka-san in his reeking rice-paddy found deep-seated satisfaction in all this activity in his behalf. His son in the army brought him a delightful sense of importance among his fellow villagers. "Tanaka-san father of a soldier of the Emperor!" Then there was the comforting sense of having a strong vocal advocate who was endeavoring to right ancient wrongs. One's fortunes were certainly looking up, except for a single important item – the price of rice. But all measures to control the economic behavior of this all-important commodity, whose price gyrations disastrously affected the entire rural economy, were unsuccessful.

Poor Tanaka-san was tied up with a group only part of whose objectives paralleled his needs. He could not know that military adventures are closely linked with securing a vast flow of foodstuffs. So Tanaka-san produced his rice and other commodities, little realizing that his military friends were doing their best to increase imports of foreign rice. For after all, what industrial and military Japan needed was an abundant supply of rice at low prices. So Tanaka-san's military friends tried to ride two wild horses, attempting to secure for Tanaka-san a high domestic price for his production, at the same time creating conditions for a low world price. They rarely succeeded in protecting Tanaka-san from the low world price.

Now of course, the military group were using Tanaka-san and his friends in the village to further their own schemes designed to plunge Japan into a war. This dismal military venture was to involve failure on a catastrophic scale, costing millions of lives and accomplishing the economic ruin of Japan.

The Farmer in World War II

By 1935 Tanaka-san found that his new friends were definitely unable to secure a satisfactory price for his products. Also, they were strangely reluctant to secure wholehearted enforcement of the many items of reform which they had sponsored in his behalf. As a matter of fact, the politicos considered that the time for reform was past. True, Tanaka-san had been an extremely useful ally in helping the

samurai-soldiers execute the political maneuvers leading to the seizure of power. But, with power in their grasp, the military were now
on the very threshold of their final objective – war itself. To this
end, all that had gone before was prelude. Tanaka-san had served one
of his two main purposes in the eyes of the militarists. His remaining value to them was as a food producer; his role as political partner
was finished.

Outright, universal enforcement of the new statutory rights for
farmers in these circumstances was politically unwise or seemed to
be. For on the eve of a major war the military needed a united people.
All cleavages must be healed in the interest of maintaining national
solidarity. Divisions of interest could not be tolerated, and the split
between landlords and their tenants, greatly widened by the military-
sponsored reforms, was one of these divisions. Gradual abandonment
of the reforms found some justification because of their implicit con-
tradiction of the feudal mythology. A case could be made that enforcement of the reforms did tend to set up an inferior against a traditional
superior and did tend to formalize a right of conflict. It was rather
simple, then, to brush aside and play down enforcement of the reforms
particularly if enforcement involved conflict. With the rising tide of
war propaganda, always accenting stern, old-fashioned samurai mo-
rality and the need for sacrifice to the Son of Heaven, it was also
simple to make a recalcitrant tenant appear out of step with the
patriotic tempo.

In spite of this, some gains, though not of immediate value, remained. An official record of the needs of agrarian reform had been
made. Recognition of principles by which reform could be accomplished was widespread. Moreover, these principles were basically
sound, and although partially inoperative, the legislation for their
execution still existed. The need for and the means of accomplishing
(1) reform of agricultural credit, (2) landlord-tenant reform, (3) limited control by farmers through cooperatives of their buying and selling requirements had thus been legally established. Tanaka-san
might have comforted himself with the thought that quite a lot of
ground had been gained.

This, in fact, proved to be the case. For war unleashed and increased the adverse forces which had borne so hard on Tanaka-san.
But now control of these forces was no longer a question of politics
but of military logic. Indeed, it seems that war often presents economic problems whose solution requires very different measures
from those required to obtain political support for starting a war.
Measures which are politically unwise for warmongers have a way of
becoming military necessities.

After 1937, several agrarian war measures of considerable severity were put in effect. Arbitration of tenant-landlord disputes became
mandatory. Eviction of tenants except in extreme cases was prohibited. Farm rentals were frozen as were land prices. These and
similar measures remained in effect throughout the entire war period.

Together with the legislation of the twenties and thirties, they represented in 1945 the body of law developed by the Japanese people for meeting the problems of the tiny farms and the toiling peasants.

By now Japan was at war, and as the war deepened, the simple life of the Japanese rural villages was caught up in the grinding grim machinery of a war economy. Everything was rationed and almost all aspects of life were strictly regimented. Village authorities were in effect agents of the imperial government. Crops were planted on order as to amount and kind. Quotas established for delivery of the crops to the authorities had to be met. Distribution of seed, fertilizer, and other items of production was geared to production quotas. Autonomous village cooperatives were succeeded by a government-run Village Association *(Nogyo Kai)* which served as a delivery and receiving point of all production goods and crop collection quotas. Payments for crops to individual farmers were set up as credits on the association books, and these were automatically drawn against by the authorities to meet all sorts of new war taxes and assessments with little or no consultation of depositors. Surplus balances, which were actually conscripted peasant savings, were forwarded to central banking agencies to meet mounting war expenses. Farmers were permitted to draw against their balances only in accord with strict regulations. In effect, the individual family lost almost completely any control whatever over its own economic life.

These measures were supplemented by continual exhortation to further sacrifices by the village bureaucracy. The mayor, the schoolmaster, the agricultural agent, the station master, the postmaster, and the policeman all became explicitly and definitively the masters of Tanaka-san. Police surveillance was meticulous. The dread *Kempei-tai* (thought police) revived the old *gonin-kumiai* (association of five families) for mutual surveillance and responsibility, with each family head responsible for the carrying out of their duties by the other four. Military needs for land, to be used for training purposes, airfields, artillery ranges, and maneuver areas, were met by ruthless expropriation of owners and cultivators with payment to be made at the end of the war. Thousands and thousands of acres of sorely needed land went for these purposes. Villages were expected to accept and shelter the large number of refugees from the war-torn cities. In addition, men needed for the army and for employment in the war industries were drafted with little or no notice and without reducing village quotas for production.

Chapter 5

WAR'S END

A S THE struggle reached its climax, the entire war effort became increasingly dependent on the efforts of the farmers. As shipping losses mounted, imports of staple from Burma, Thailand, Formosa, the Philippines, and the South Pacific fell steadily. Cultivators were urged to greater and greater efforts. With the multiplication of disasters, the appeals for production became more frantic. Sterner and sterner methods were taken to enforce them.

But American might waxed ever greater and moved inexorably closer. The merchant fleet disappeared. The navy began to disintegrate, as sinkings far outran decreasing power to replace lost and damaged vessels. One by one at first, and later by whole groups, the Solomons, the Marshalls, the Mariannas, and the Carolines were lost. Each loss meant the lopping off of a segment of the army which could not be replaced. There were no wounded and no retreating troops to re-form and re-group, only the dead, on the beaches, in the jungles, and under the sea.

Then the entire South Pacific and all the hopes its conquest had aroused were gone; cleared completely of Japanese ships, planes, and men. The Philippines were invaded and Manila fell. Guam's capture was followed by bloody Iwo Jima and the terrible Okinawa campaign. The final agony commenced. Young men, after a night of ghastly celebration and ceremonial, were strapped into light planes whose undercarriage dropped away in the take-off of a flight which ended in a burst of flame on the deck of some American transport or in a mighty geyser of smoke, sea water, and wreckage. But these and other acts of suicidal bravery were not enough.

War on the Home Islands

In small groups at first and later in vast numbers the armadas of B-29 bombers appeared over Japan itself. Their missions of flame and destruction must have seemed endless to people who endured them. In the beginning some were shot down, but their greater power finally saturated the ground defenses. Nor was the air defense itself able to cope with their terrific fire power. Tokyo and Yokohama were repeatedly engulfed in flames and the adjoining vast industrial area became a tangled mass of wreckage – a scene of indescribable chaos

and ruin. A similar fate befell all the other industrial areas: the
vital shipping, trading, and manufacturing complex of Osaka, Kobe,
and the Hanchin cities that lay in a narrow coastal strip under the
hills of Hyogo; the great aircraft center of Nagoya; the steel mills
of Yawata; the great naval base at Kure. Sometimes the fires burned
for days completely out of control and the people fled before them into
the open country.

In retrospect, it is remarkable that so little disorganization occurred. Wherever possible, affairs proceeded in normal patterns of
life. Families moved to the countryside, husbands remaining behind
or commuting regularly to their jobs from the new dwellings. Com-
muter trains would stop from time to time as planes appeared so the
passengers could seek safety under the cars or in the fields until the
immediate danger had passed. So life and business went on as usual.
When this was no longer possible, a makeshift facsimile was attempted.
Thus a front of normalcy was preserved although fleets of ships were
sunk with no survivors, whole armies vanished almost without trace,
and the homeland lay helpless under the hammer blows from the air.

In the fields, the small brown farmer folk bent to their work. Demands on them had become fantastic. Yet it must have seemed that
every sacrifice and extra exertion was offset by a greater catastrophe.
But who knows what they thought or felt? There is no record of protest or of sorrow. As their burdens multiplied, their sons, brothers,
and fathers left the village to disappear wordlessly and forever in the
pall of smoke and flame of an industrial center, in the waters of the
Pacific, or to recede into the vast silences of Manchuria and Siberia,
leaving no trace.

The production of food reached a critical stage. Moreover, only
the production on the home islands remained to feed the people and
their armies. So, the increasing demand for food was met with an
ever dwindling ability to produce it. In 1945, the monthly average
production of chemical fertilizers, including ammonium sulphate and
calcium cynamide, fell to less than a third of the 1940 output. Not
only was the folume of food production measurably lowered but its
nutritive value decreased as the diet became more and more confined
to straight carbohydrates. Moreover, increasing demands for industrial and military manpower were often met by drafts on the rural
labor force. A smaller remaining force of older men were called on
to do a larger and larger job. Refugees, largely children and women,
from the bombed-out areas flooded the countryside and were billeted
as best they could be. Village housing was crowded with female relations and their offspring.

A new phase of landlord-tenant relations commenced. Landlords,
long absent from the village, returned. They sought both greater
safety and an assured food supply. Many sought to evict their tenants,
to "return to their land" as the Japanese express it. Their metropolitan business was at a standstill. They faced the uncertainties of
getting food through a crippled distribution system. So farming, long

despised, now assumed a most desirable aspect for the erstwhile
absentee landlords. Access to land seemed the only sure means of
avoiding starvation. As this fact became more evident, tenant evictions spread and were more and more ruthlessly carried out. With
too many other things on their minds, the authorities could ill afford,
in the last months of the war, to spend time enforcing legal safeguards
for tenants, particularly when the displacement released sorely needed
recruits for the factory or the army.

These were some of the disabilities under which the villagers
struggled. In addition, the government, beset on all sides, was less
and less able to enforce its price controls and inflation appeared. It
was still easy to force the peasant to disgorge his harvest, but it was
almost impossible to provide him the things he needed at controlled
prices. Black markets flourished and increased in scope. Price
offenders were difficult to detect and harder still to prosecute.

As the rural economic fabric frayed, the farmer staggered under
his load. The total acreage under cultivation shrunk and yields
dropped and dropped. By 1945, as a result of accumulated fertilizer
deficiencies and inadequate labor, the average yields of several staple
crops were the lowest in nearly forty years. This condition spelled
starvation and clearly foretold the disastrous end of the wretched
military adventure so auspiciously undertaken thirteen years before.
For once in its history the rulers of Japan had pushed the peasants
beyond the limit of their powers.

So the final hour approached. Village headmen passed on instructions from higher authority for the defense of the home islands.
Clumsy pill boxes were erected under the directions of civilian authorities. Some of them, still visible in 1947, looked like oversized
white bee hives. Caves were dug in the hillsides as a final fortifica-
tion, if the villages should be lost. A home guard of old men and
adolescents were armed with bamboo spears. It is rumored that in
some instances poison was distributed among the womenfolk so that
they might, with honor, escape rape by the terrible invaders.

Futile and even clumsily humorous as these measures seem now,
the Japanese meant seriously and determinedly to follow them to the
end. One can only imagine the horror which would have ensued if this
program and the counsel on which it was based had prevailed. American troops would have been forced into a prolonged campaign ending
only with annihilation of almost the entire Japanese population.

But even as the officials made ready for this last stand, there
came the utterly shattering news of Hiroshima and Nagasaki. Many
Japanese have told me that up to that point they had sometimes been
dispirited and often sad, but had never known sheer terror. Now, in
spite of strict censorship, word of the atomic holocaust spread. To
many the ensuing days were a period of complete despair. So dreadful was this period that the radio announcement in the unmistakable
tones of their own Emperor proclaiming the end of the war, the end of
resistance, the end of the Japanese Empire, must have seemed almost

a glad reprieve. A ruined, starving nation had fallen after a bitter
war. One imagines that, mingled with the crash of the collapse, ran
a central theme which signified the end of a whole way of life, a
structure of tradition, and a code of social existence.

Capitulation

The end of summer ushers in the typhoon season in the Western
Pacific. But we may suppose the weather was clear enough for peo-
ple in surrounding fields and hills to have seen the vast flights of
American planes and the great grim battleship "Missouri," as she
lay in the Tokyo Bay on that fateful day early in September, 1945.
The officials of the Japanese surrender party on her main deck faced
Douglas MacArthur, their official conqueror, and Jonathan Wainwright,
their ex-prisoner. One imagines General MacArthur's expression
was stern, reflecting a determination as inflexible as that of the other
American, Commodore Matthew Galbraith Perry of South Kingstown in
Rhode Island. A space of just over 92 years separated the encounter
of these two great American captains with their Japanese opponents,
in Tokyo Bay – MacArthur in 1945 on the formidable "Missouri,"
Perry in 1853 on the "Susquehanna," described by the Japanese as
"a black ship of evil mien." Yet each brought to the people of those
islands doctrines whose introduction meant in each case a new way of
life and a new political direction. Perry ended two centuries of complete isolation and so helped release forces which created a Japanese
Empire. The Terms of Surrender signed in 1945 ended the Japanese
Empire and established the revolutionary principle of individual liberty
among the Japanese.

The people on hillsides above the bay and in fields alongside it
waited with all the other people in all fields and cities of Japan to hear
the orders of the conqueror. Told by their own Emperor of his decision to surrender the Empire and of the need for their cooperation
with the victorious occupying army and its Commander, they prepared
to accept their new destiny.

The terms were simple, largely reaffirming on the part of Japan
her adherence to the general principles laid down the preceding July
in the Potsdam Declaration. This document proclaimed the decision
of the Allies that "the time has come for Japan to decide whether she
will continue to be controlled by those self-willed militaristic advisors
whose unintelligent calculations have brought the Empire of Japan to
the threshold of annihilation or whether she will follow the path of
reason." But the Declaration also contained, for a nation so long
wedded to principles of autocracy and human inequality and tyranny of
government, the sweeping and revolutionary principle that "the Japanese Government shall remove all obstacles to the revival and strengthening of democratic tendencies among the Japanese people. Freedom
of speech, of religion, and of thought, as well as respect for the fundamental human rights shall be established." In effect, the terms of

surrender expressed the intention of displacing and upsetting a great
part of the structure of custom and law which had for so long dominated the life of the peasantry of Japan.

Meeting the Food-Shortage Crisis

There was much to be done. The job could be clearly visualized
and means to do it were at hand. Surely no thinking individual view-
ing the scene could escape the challenge of a great opportunity and of
a responsibility of equal magnitude. It was the latter which initially
made urgent claims on the attention of the newly arrived authorities.
For Japan, surrendering almost at the last gasp, was a ruined country
with a vast population on the verge of starvation.

It was necessary to move and move fast if a catastrophe were to
be averted. The first problem was food. How to get it? How to collect it? How to distribute it? So almost at the outset, the new
framers of Japanese state policy encountered once again the age-old
problem of combining food supply and government.

The challenge to the occupying powers which this situation presented was primarily of avoiding starvation and economic chaos.
Since the 1945 crop had already been harvested, no relief from indigenous Japanese production could be expected until the 1946 harvest.
So the problem of feeding hungry people could be separated into two
parts – first, of meeting the immediate crisis and second, of planning
a program for maximizing agricultural production over a long period.
The only immediate solution to the current food problem was through
a completely efficient mobilization and distribution of all available
food resources. This required fairly drastic controls both at the
village collection points and in distribution channels. Even so, it was
apparent that food would have to be imported from abroad. The deficit
was made up by direct imports from the United States and by foreign
purchases largely financed with American dollars.

With these emergency measures quickly designed by the agricultural technicians of the Occupation, the Japanese were able to get
through the fall of 1945 and the winter and spring of 1946. Although
outright starvation was avoided by a narrow margin, everyone was
hungry and life was utterly wretched.   There was considerable malnutrition, and if statistics were available, the number of deaths
directly and indirectly attributable to this cause would probably have
shown a considerable rise. The tuberculosis death rate did show a
sharp increase and the number of cases of nine dangerous infectious
diseases grew to disturbing proportions. Among the youth of the
country, growth measured in weight and height showed a marked decrease between 1937 and 1945. Neither the average diet nor the
basic health of the people offered encouragement in the immediate
situation.

Starvation and disease were allayed by prompt, efficiently enforced
emergency measures and by direct aid, mostly from the United States.

But the long range stability of food supply depended on a careful adjustment of production factors. Principal among these factors were the producers themselves. As an emergency measure to avoid imminent disaster, farmers could be forced to deliver up larger and larger portions of everything they produced and to plant according to an enforced plan. In the long run, such a program could not be reconciled with the mission of the Occupation.

Ultimately, increased food production would have to result from the free will of the peasants. Hence, long-range planning for increments in agricultural production had to seek such instrumentalities as improved techniques, increased fertilizer production, a better ratio between commodity prices and prices to farmers for nonfarm goods, and finally an economic and social framework in which incentive and initiative could be free to function. Thus, concern with food supply, both as an emergency problem and as an element in long-range economic policy, led to a close examination by the Occupation of the entire rural economy.

Chapter 6

POST SURRENDER JAPAN
AND THE AGRARIAN PROBLEM

IN THE interval immediately following the surrender, the military Occupation of Japan had proceeded swiftly and according to plan. The headquarters of the Supreme Commander of the Allied Powers, General MacArthur, was set up in Tokyo. A short distance away, at Yokohama, was the headquarters of the Eighth United States Army, commanded by General Eichelberger. Two corps headquarters were established, one for North Japan at Sendai in Miyagi prefecture, the other two hundred odd miles south of Tokyo at Kyoto for Central and Southwestern Japan. Teams composed of officers trained for military government were stationed in the capital of each of the 46 prefectures. Prefectural military government terms were controlled by the corps headquarters. These functioned under Eighth Army Command. General Headquarters in Tokyo established the over-all policies through directives which were put into effect by Eighth Army.

Patterns and policy for the Occupation worked out among the Allies were transmitted to General MacArthur as orders by the Joint Chiefs of Staff. The initial and perhaps most important Occupation document issued by this group was the Basic Directive for Post Surrender Military Government in Japan Proper, issued on November 3, 1945. This document interpreted the broad principles of the Potsdam Declaration and the Terms of Surrender in their application to the major subdivisions of Japanese economy and society. It specified the powers of the Supreme Commander and the general measures to be taken for the enforcement of the Allied Policy.

All forms of militarism and ultranationalism were to be abolished. Democratic tendencies and processes in governmental, economic, and social institutions were to be strengthened. Changes modifying feudal and authoritarian tendencies of government were to be introduced. The principle of local responsibility for the enforcement of national policy was to be favored as was development of democratic organizations in labor, industry, and agriculture. Policies were to be inaugurated which would "encourage the development within Japan of economic ways and institutions that will contribute to the growth of peaceful and democratic forces in Japan." Economic arrangements and operations were to be so guided that they would conform to these purposes. The Japanese government was to be required to make such changes in the structure of government administration as seemed necessary to the Supreme Commander to carry out those objectives.

Specific mention was made of the need for avoiding economic distress and for equitable distribution of available supplies. No person was to be permitted to take or retain an important or influential position in industry, finance, commerce, or agriculture who had been an exponent of militant nationalism and aggression. Policies were to be followed which would "permit a wide distribution of income and of ownership of the means of production and trade."

This document and his military organization gave to General MacArthur both the general policy which he was to follow and the machinery for executing it. In the case of the agricultural economy something was known of the specific problems to be encountered. During their training period, Military Government personnel had received considerable information about Japan's agriculture. Moreover, the headquarters staff contained trained professional agricultural personnel. Literature on Japanese agriculture which had found its way into the English language was scant. Nevertheless, available literature plus official studies made by the Office of Foreign Agriculture Relations of the United States Department of Agriculture stressed the Japanese land situation and the concomitant tenant problem as one of the basic ills of Japan.

Even before the war, members of Ambassador Grew's staff had recorded their observations of the economic unsoundness and social inequity of the tenant system. An Australian political scientist, Dr. W. MacMahan Ball of Melbourne, put it well: "The emancipation of the peasant must be the first and most important step in any programme for the economic and spiritual emancipation of the Japanese people. Nearly half of the Japanese people live in farm households. Their importance lies not only in these numbers, but in the fact that they represent what is most backward in Japanese society. Much more than any other class they show the spirit and habits of feudalism. No democracy can be built on a foundation of agricultural feudalism."

To a considerable degree, emancipation of the peasants signified a reform of Japan's land tenure system and of tenancy. Thus from several directions Occupation interest converged on problems of the Japanese peasant. Experience with the actual food emergency pointed to need for a stable agricultural economy which required in turn a more suitable adjustment between land resources and rural population. Students and observers of the Japanese scene almost without exception cited the need for a reform of rural institutions. Finally, the documents of surrender and of Occupation established criteria in contrast with which the existing agrarian complex was glaringly deficient.

First Contacts With Americans

At the top level of policy and authority, relations between Americans and Japanese were stiff and formal. Feelings were colored perhaps, on the part of Americans, by suspicion; on the part of Japanese, by fear. But at the village level things were a good deal easier.

Perhaps it was the children who served as unwitting emissaries between their elders and the big foreigners. Big-eyed with wonder, they stared speechlessly at the first American soldiers. Never in their lives before had these young men from California, Iowa, New York, and Georgia been such centers of wordless concentrated attention. Everything — their jeeps, their clothes, their weapons, and their gestures — all were the object of closest scrutiny, of utter, silent fascination. Attempts at communication by the Americans accompanied by offers of chocolate or chewing gum increased the dimensions of the audience. As a military vehicle entered the village and halted, a silent message seemed to signal the entire juvenile population. Smaller children broke away from their mothers to join the throng. Sometimes a block or two distant little boys ran on their clattering *geta*, stubby legs churning desperately, to join the growing throng made up of every age from the infant strapped on the six-year-old sister's back to boys in their early teens.

Even in remote villages the English words, "hello" and "chocolate" — "Herro" and "Chokaratu" — became a part of almost every child's vocabulary. These initial fraternizations led to a casual word or two with a parent, a return gift of flowers from an older woman in behalf of a gum-endowed urchin, and finally to a brief visit to the house. From these preliminaries the establishment of complete informal liaison between the G.I.s and rural people was a simple matter.

Japan is a small country and it didn't take long for the Americans to be visible at one time or another in almost all its villages. For several weeks after the surrender these newcomers must have seemed to the peasants to be the only evidence of the Occupation — along with the tightened and more rigorous black market control measures which local officials were not slow to tell them originated with the Americans.

Nevertheless, whether they knew it or not, these rural people and their affairs were receiving very close attention from very important people. For the first time the rural population segment was being viewed, not as an instrument of state policy, but as composed of human beings with lives and rights of their own. For the first time in Japanese history the structure of superior-inferior social relations in the village was being questioned. For the first time the issue was raised as to whether agricultural production could not be better achieved by free peasant proprietors, with a voice in their own destiny, rather than by regimentation.

Occupation Policy and the Tenancy Problem

It became daily more certain that a complete reorganization of the agrarian economy was essential to any national program of democratization. The controls to which the peasants had been so long

accustomed represented the very antithesis of the political principles
which the Occupation aimed to establish. So a reform of rural life
was indispensable to sweeping away the structure of military rule
which had made the Japanese a nation of obedient puppets. As long as
agrarian Japan remained in thralldom, it would constitute a lever susceptible of domination by undemocratic leaders to coerce all other
segments of society.

It was also clear that a key factor in the agrarian structure was
the tenure system which subjugated toiling tenants to the will of the
landlords. These nonproducers could enforce the feudal code of inequality through their grip on the vital element of land. Control of
land equalled control of the peasants. This in turn meant control of
food production. In a country where the margin of nutrition was so
slender, control of food conveyed automatically ability to dominate the
entire society. Vested land control was therefore a political tool.

But this land tenure system could exist only in an atmosphere con-
genial to continued recognition of traditional authority. Basically the
tenancy system was not well adapted to the natural land resources nor
to the needs of the community. Fundamentally, therefore, its stability
depended on extension of controls, not on adjustment between resources
and needs. With the disasters of the war all these traditional sources
of control were severely shaken.

In actual fact, a whole constellation of Japanese symbols had fallen
into disrepute. Japanese villagers were, as a matter of sober thought,
considering how the gods which had brought them to the brink of ruin
might be replaced with others more harmonious with realities of defeat. So, too, with the traditional loyalties.

Consider the inherent confusion and attendant insecurity which must
have tortured the peasants of the Japanese village as they watched
the long columns of Occupation troops roll by. Mingling sensations of
fascination, curiosity, and terror must have shaken them. They beheld
their youngsters in amiable relations with these large, confident young
men who were patently friendly but openly unabashed in the presence
of century-old traditions and constituted authority. They saw the
headmen casually questioned and responding courteously, even obse-
quiously. There was no hint of violence or of hate but rather a careless disregard of established leaders, which was psychologically even
more shattering to confidence. When the village policemen punctili-
ously rendered their best military salutes to the tall, casual young non-
coms as they sauntered in the village streets, they were answered
if at all, with a careless wave. Yet such indifference was a terrific
shock to long-held sentiments of respect and awe.

In this light, the peasantry, with very little at stake, was slowly
coming to an awareness that the forces which had confined them within
a tight pattern of behavior were no longer so powerful. Obedience was
a sort of involuntary reflex, but the compulsive authority which evoked
it was waning fast. For want of a substitute, perhaps, the old ways
continued to be observed. But it was clear that the situation was

unstable. Some answer satisfactory to the needs and aspirations of agrarian life must be provided soon.

In retrospect, the speed with which the essentials of this problem were grasped by Occupation authorities should evoke respect. Less than 60 days after the surrender the problems of agrarian Japan were being vigorously attacked by an extraordinarily able group of professional agricultural scientists. In this period, personnel of the Supreme Commander's headquarters were sleeping and eating as best they could amidst the ruins of Tokyo. Places to work and conduct business were being established in makeshift quarters. Even in the beginning, while the immediate emergency of feeding the Japanese out of the distressingly short food supply was being met, the groundwork of longer range policy and action was being laid.

The State Department furnished General MacArthur a comprehensive outline of the farm tenancy situation. Although this document was based largely on prewar observations, nevertheless it displayed a commendable comprehension of the need for a vigorous reorganization of land tenure arrangements and suggested a number of ways for effecting it. The report agreed with observations of Dr. W. MacMahon Ball that reasonably prosperous conditions and peaceful tendencies could not prevail in Japan without agrarian reforms. Removal of an inequitable tenancy system was an indispensable requirement of such a reform.

General MacArthur's prompt favorable response to these proposals was fortunate. The specific concern with the details of this work which the Supreme Commander displayed, his comprehension of technical problems of agriculture and particularly of the complex land tenure situation were refreshing. His enthusiasm was an essential factor in enabling his technical staff successfully to attack the formidable complex of problems, vested interest, and tradition which the Japanese rural economy presented. To those immediately concerned, the General's interest in and support of their work will remain as an outstanding part of the Allied Occupation of Japan.

Largely because of the perception of the Supreme Commander the reform of rural institutions of Japan was given a central position in Occupation policy. In its recognition of the key importance of agriculture and of farm people this attitude gave a stature and renown to American policy that reached beyond the confines of Japan because of its profound significance to all of Asia. For in Asia the overwhelming majority of the people are farmers and the characteristic problems of the entire Asiatic continent are those of people who seek a living from the land. No policy for Asia which fails to accord a central place to agrarian affairs has a chance of success since it then lacks content and significance to the mass of the population.

So the handful of agricultural specialists in General MacArthur's headquarters dug out the details of the land tenure situation and of other significant aspects of the rural economy. What a gruelling task it was! The sources of information were in the terribly difficult written or spoken Japanese language. American personnel had received considerable drill in Japanese, but since any adequate mastery of the language requires years of intensive effort, their linguistic ability was completely inadequate for all but the simplest conversations. Consequently, the task of fact finding was complicated by a dearth of adequate interpreters of the written and spoken word. Some of the information was in the research records of principal universities, of course in Japanese. Some material was in back numbers of technical journals and in the agricultural sections of 46 prefectural governments scattered over Japan.

Valuable assistance came from several Japanese agricultural scholars, veterans of the long struggle to reform Japanese agriculture who had barely escaped the attentions of the thought police and imprisonment. All had known hardships during the war and were in wretched circumstances. However, their qualifications and attitude were good. They had received sound graduate training in Europe and America. They knew where reliable information was located – or rather where it had been located, for of course libraries and statistical files like everything else had been bombed and burned.

A number of other events more immediately dramatic than the work of the agricultural section of the headquarters had taken place in September and October, 1945. The "surrender" Cabinet of Prince Higashi-Kuni formed in August to negotiate Japan's capitulation resigned en bloc on October 5. It was immediately succeeded by the interim government of Baron Kijuro Shidehara which ran the country until the general elections in the spring of 1946. The terrific loss of face caused by the abortive suicide attempt of General Tojo on September 11 deeply shocked the nation, as did the arrest of 38 Japanese leaders as war criminals the same day. On the next day the double suicide of Field Marshal Sugiyama and his wife occurred. Simultaneously the Japanese Military Headquarters was dissolved.

The disruption and destruction of dictatorship proceeded. On September 22, all censorship controls of newspapers and news agencies were removed. On October 4, a day to be remembered by many, the Supreme Commander ordered the liberation of all political prisoners. Abolition of the secret police and removal of the Home Minister in charge of all police activities, as well as abrogation and immediate suspension of wartime laws followed. On October 31, immediate dismissal from all educational work of militarists and ultranationalists was ordered. Thus, by the end of October informed Japanese could foresee that action in any direction by the Occupation was likely to be sweeping, drastic, and directed toward reform of existing inequities.

Japanese Resistance to Allied Policy

It was not hard for the Japanese leadership to detect the trend of Allied thought on agrarian affairs. The exhaustive interviews between

American and Japanese agricultural specialists and the direction of
the research concentrated on prevailing land tenure arrangements
foretold sweeping demands for agrarian reform. Now, although the
Shidehara government contained no war criminals, it did contain –
both in the cabinet and the Diet – many individuals with close ties to
land. In most instances these persons were closely allied with the
landlord interest. These political leaders must have recognized that
no reform to the land system could take place without greatly affecting
the landlords. They could foresee the need for prompt action if sweeping changes were not to be imposed.

In former years the vested landlord interest had forestalled the
rising political tide of agrarian reform and with considerable success.
Consequently the group was not at all inexperienced. It had achieved
in prior years a close unity of purpose and an understanding of tactics.
Moreover, the group was even more deeply aware than the Americans
of the vital role of agriculture as an element of political control. Many
in this group of politicians still regarded Japan as a nation of destiny.
Perhaps they regarded the loss of the war as a major defeat to their
semispiritual ambitions for an Asiatic hegemony under Japanese
leadership. Nevertheless, after the fashion of such men, it seems
probable that they regarded the setback, however drastic, as an inter-
ruption to, but not the end of, their ambitions.

But control of the land and of food was a vital part of any plans for
control of Japan's destiny. Hence the Occupation interest in agriculture and particularly in land aroused their keenest attention. Apparently a coterie around Shidehara began to lay plans to counteract the
Occupation's most probable course of action in rural affairs. The
reaction of this group and its subsequent activities are worth mention-
ing since they give added insight to the crucial importance of land in any
strategy for the political orientation of Japan.

By early November, 1945, the problem which the Occupation technicians had been attempting to formulate was stated in this fashion:
"What specific changes in the prevailing social and economic structure
of Japanese agriculture are necessary to make it conform to Occupation policy?" Having stated a problem, the argument then took the
form of a series of specific recommendations with regard to various
phases of that structure. The final step was to reduce these to the
draft of a directive to be issued to the Japanese government.

The Japanese political leaders, aware that the Occupation would in
all probability seek a major reform of the tenure system, set out to
develop independent tenure reform legislation. Perhaps they hoped to
produce their own legislation prior to the formal issuance of Occupation demands. In that case, they may have anticipated that agrarian
matters would possibly be left entirely in their hands. Perhaps they
believed that, even if formal demands for reform were issued, their
legislation might be accepted as satisfactory compliance. It is quite
likely that some were motivated purely by national pride, preferring
to have their own legislation, voluntarily enacted, rather than be
forced to enact legislation under compulsion. The latter probability is
strengthened by its very apparent appeal to face-saving.

Another factor prompting the Japanese to devise a land reform scheme was undoubtedly due to pressure from perfectly sincere agrarian reformers. These reform-minded men were genuinely unselfish. Possibly they were a little naive and unfamiliar with political maneuvering. They may have been prone, as loyal Japanese, to settle for less than the full price likely to be demanded by the Occupation. At any rate, some of these well-meaning men seem to have been persuaded of the need for moderation and for modification of a sweeping reform as a *quid pro quo* in securing necessary political support.

The effect of all these crosscurrents was a precipitate effort to forestall Occupation action on the land question. This action culminated in an announcement on November 23, 1945, by the Shidehara government of its intention to enact land reform legislation immediately. This announcement was prominently featured by the Japanese press. But it was an intention that had not been kept entirely secret from certain interests. This leakage of information was evidenced by a sudden increase in the number of evictions of tenants by absentee landlords just prior to the announcement. Motivation for these evictions, of course, lay in well-justified fears that any reform, whether originating from Japanese or Occupation sources, could hardly fail to make some adjustment in the status of *absentee* ownership. So a number of well-informed absentee landlords betook themselves to the site of their land, hoping by the maneuver to appear legally as genuine cultivators in the event of worst coming to worst.

This government maneuver in announcing a land reform program must be credited with cleverness. It was an adroit counterplay which clearly indicated that, although defeated, the Japanese were still capable adversaries. Perhaps if the Americans had been less zealous in assembling facts about rural conditions, or less intelligent in integrating them in cogent conclusions, or, indeed, if the Occupation as a whole had been less firmly devoted to the principles it advocated, the scheme might have been more successful. As it was, the work of documentation and preparation of necessary official action to reform the agrarian structure of Japan, particularly the land tenure system, proceeded steadily and without reference to the independent action of Shidehara. The completed study, a plan for action, and the draft of proposed orders to the Japanese government were transmitted to General MacArthur on December 5, 1945.

The Land Reform Directive

Four days later the General issued his famous Land Reform Directive, expressed in drastic language, admirable for its brevity. The order in effect canceled the existing tenancy system of Japan and ordered the substitution of a new system based on the ownership of land by those who had cultivated it. The government was required on or before March 15, 1946, to submit to the Headquarters a program of rural land reform which would remove obstacles to democracy and destroy economic bondage in rural areas. The Government plan must contain the following provisions: (1) transfer of land ownership from absentee land owners to land operators, (2) purchase of farm lands from any non-operating owner at equitable rates, (3) sale of land to tenants at annual installments commensurate with tenant income, and (4) protection of former tenants who purchased land against reversion to tenancy status. The directive further warned that its purpose was to *uproot* and *destroy* the various evils which had for so long blighted the lives of the peasantry. Tenancy was to be destroyed and landlordism must cease to exist.

This order was tantamount to an open avowal of one central purpose: destruction of feudal social relations in Japanese villages and removal of agricultural production as an element of economic support of the political power of autocratic government. If this program succeeded, a really complete shift of power in the Japanese state was inevitable.

In spite of the simple wording of this Occupation directive and the definitive nature of its requirements, Japanese lawmakers went ahead with preparation of the legislation announced by their communiqué of November 23, 1945. Headquarters officials let them know informally that their proposed legislation did not meet the requirements of the Supreme Commander's directive. Nevertheless, the legislation was passed by the Diet on December 18, 1945, and promulgated ten days later. Even though short of meeting Allied requirements, the measure itself was considerably more stringent in its impact on the landlords than any previous Japanese land reform legislation.

Thus at the end of 1945, four months after surrender, the Japanese land tenure system was under attack by both the Japanese government and the Occupation. It was apparent therefore that in any event existing landlord-tenant relations were in for a revision, less drastic if the Japanese version prevailed, very sweeping if General MacArthur stood by his declaration. Thus landlords and tenants in 11,000 communities were now officially on notice that a change was coming, a change favorable to tenants, adverse to landlords.

Chapter 7

LAND REFORM BECOMES LAW

THE splendid blue fall days of 1945 brightened and sharpened into
the dry, cold winter season of 1946. The graceful black veined
cone of Fuji, so aptly described by Hearn, hung like a half-opened
fan from the crystalline sky.[1] In the drab grey villages misery and
hunger deepened. Runny-nosed children squatted apathetically in temple yards, occasionally smearing their oppressed noses on the sleeves
of padded kimonos. Parents told the boys they were "from the wind"
so were expected to endure cold. But older people were "from fire"
so explaining the need to squat before smoky charcoal embers in the
large earthenware pots *(hibachi)* comfortlessly warming their hands
and torsos. The combination of cold, hunger, and early dark was now
unrelieved by electric light. Sickness and the weakness of semistarva-
tion increased the insecurity resulting from impending changes in village relations now accented by announcement of impending reform of
the land system.

But if the landless tenants felt any joy at the prospective change in
their fortunes, they kept it to themselves. The matter went far too
deep for any idle or casual expression. A tenant farmer with a family
of ten in Kyoto Fu, whose total harvest was 75 bushels of rice and
whose rent was 45 bushels, professed no personal interest in the matter of land reform. There was 66-year-old Sakuichi Fukuda of Bofu
Shi in Yamaguchi ken in southwest Honshu. Fukuda, a grandfather
with a son lost in the South Pacific, was now responsible for a family
of eight. He cultivated about two and a quarter acres, giving 60 per
cent of his crops as rent. When questioned about land reform, this
elderly tenant expressed only the kindest sentiments toward his landlord saying he was "a very nice man" and that he would be "very
sorry" for him if he lost his land.

In fact, we of the Occupation back in Tokyo were learning very
quickly and with considerable misgiving that the Japanese were a deal
more complex than they appeared. We soon perceived that the administration of land reform involved a number of factors not included in

---

[1]Cf. Lafcadio Hearn, *Exotics and Retrospectives* (Boston: Little, Brown, and Co., 1898),
p. 3: "...you perceive only the white cone seeming to hang in heaven; and the Japanese
comparison of its shape to an inverted half-open fan is made wonderfully exact by the five
streaks that spread downward from the notched top, like shadows of fan-ribs."

any formulas for economic equity. Indeed, when it came to a test between the desire for land ownership and a clear break with tradition, there seemed to be a possibility that the peasants might forego the former. Lafcadio Hearn labored hard and perhaps not too clearly to impress on Westerners the quality of the Japanese character. He termed the matured Japanese code of individual conduct "The Rule of the Dead."[2] The phrase was intended to express perhaps the strength of tradition and custom in guiding Japanese affairs.

For to Westerners the Japanese seem to display a strange mixture of sentimentality, mysticism, and realism. Promontories high over the breaking seas have to be guarded by the police because of their invitation to the execution of lovers' suicide pacts. Otherwise calm and dignified elderly gentlemen and ladies kneel composedly before the alcove of the family gods and disembowel themselves for a reason so obscure that Westerners fail to grasp its significance. Again, a famous artist draws a series of innocuous pictures whose charm is their cabalistic reference to still another famous artist's series of pictures, which in turn have veiled reference to affairs of the ancient court. The sensitivity of the Japanese to beauty and to their own notions of dignity and proper behavior is beyond anything the Westerner can touch and extends to almost all Japanese. The radiant female deity of Mt. Fuji is Ko-no-hana-saku-ya-hime, "radiant-blooming-as-the-flowers-of-the-trees,"[3] and other objects have names evoking equally sentimental association.

But in the most cherished Japanese poetic expressions the veiled meaning is perhaps the most characteristic feature; mist, not lucidity is the objective. "Too lightly woven must the garment be — garment of mist — that clothes the coming spring." One of the Hojo regents in the 13th century, Tokiyori, once welcomed a great Buddhist teacher thus enigmatically to his house in Kamakura:

> "Swollen is the stream brimming the banks
> after the vernal shower,
> Green are now the water weeds greener than the moss
> Here no one comes to the little hut
> But the gateway opens by itself when the
> Wind alone makes a visit."

The coming of spring signifies welcome and timeliness. A high compliment is intended in comparing the revered visitor with the wind, while the comparison of a ruler's palace to a hut is commonplace Japanese courtesy.[4] Yet all this emotional sensitivity stands in contrast to a tough, almost ruthless realism. There is gentleness among Japanese, but also there is hardness. There is affection, but at times there is callous indifference to suffering.

---

[2]Lafcadio Hearn, *Japan — An Attempt at Interpretation* (New York: The Macmillan Co., 1910), p. 175.

[3]Lafcadio Hearn, *Exotics and Retrospectives*, p.5.

[4]The two quotations and the interpretation are from Masaharu Anezaki's *Art, Life, and Nature in Japan* (Boston: Marshall Jones Co., 1932), pp. 12, 108, 109.

It was these mingled aspects of the Japanese spirit – mysticism, sentimentality, practicality – which were now exposed in the villages to the play and interplay of emotions by the land proposals. The struggle for actual possession of land would not even be suggested by most tenants until the formidable challenge of ethics in terms of *Yamato-damashi,* the soul of old Japan, had been resolved.[5]

Unfortunately, all these honored traditions and the mysticism which surrounded them gave landlords an immediate advantage. Some of them were descendants of samurai and under the code, formerly prevailing, a samurai was free to cut down with his sword any peasant whose behavior in the samurai's eyes was unseemly. Such ancestral sanctions gave landlords freedom of action, whereas tenants could only watch and wait.

Weakness in Japanese Legislative System

If a confused and strained emotional atmosphere prevailed in the villages, certainly the situation in Japanese government circles in Tokyo was far from serene. In passing "the first Land Reform Law" the lawmakers had overplayed their hand in attempting to outmaneuver the Occupation. In effect they had a law on their hands of which the Occupation technicians advised them they held no high opinion.

Of course, the Japanese statesmen still had until March 15, 1946, to present a plan for land reform which would satisfy General Mac-Arthur's demands. But in order to save face they must present the December 28, 1945, law which they now knew would not be adequate. A rejection of this law would create for them a pretty mess indeed. Truly they had the proverbial bear by the proverbial tail! If they attempted to enforce their own law, they could have no assurance that all acts taken under it might not have to be rescinded in a few weeks. If they did not enforce this law, the question of why it had been passed at all required an answer. Moreover, the behavior of some landlords in anticipation of its enforcement appeared likely to embarrass them still more. Then there was the humiliating circumstance of having brought it all on themselves. For the Occupation made very clear its intention to refrain from direct interference in matters of government. Its work was to be done through established government channels. Thus the Occupation position was highly strategic – all laws, including those required by the Supreme Commander, would be enacted, promulgated, and enforced by the Japanese themselves. Japanese leadership would have to take full responsibility for its acts.

If the government took thought about their relative position in the scheme of things, its members must have had serious misgivings. Japanese respect for parliamentary procedure was small. The position of the Diet and the Cabinet in the traditional structure of Japanese government had never been very strong. Both had been dominated

---

[5]Lafcadio Hearn, *Japan – An Attempt at Interpretation*, p. 177.

from above by the terrific mystic power of the Emperor and his court.
Moreover, the parliamentary machinery had been directly manipulated
in recent years by the military junta. Its opportunities to develop any
strong sense of responsibility or particular skill in governing under
conditions other than complete authoritarianism had been very limited.

Now, however, Japanese statesmen found themselves out in front.
They stood in the full spotlight of public view. They were, moreover,
fully responsible in the eyes of the Occupation. The Emperor re-
nounced his divinity on New Year's Day. The great military leaders
had disappeared into obscure countryside retreats, into prison to
await trial on war crimes charges, or into eternity by way of self-
inflicted death. In fact, in the situation which was rapidly developing,
these men of the Shidehara government were finding it more and more
necessary to look to themselves for guidance and judgment. It seems
never to have occurred to most of these statesmen to seek support
from the only remaining element in the political situation – the people. Indeed, to some Americans at the time, it seemed that the government feared, with almost superstitious terror, the concept of a
constituency to which they might be considered responsible.

Thus there was real danger that, unless very gently handled, the
government, feeling the burden of responsibility too great, might re-
fuse to act at all except on explicit detailed instructions from the
Occupation. The implications of such an abdication entailed the subsequent assumption of full responsibility for all government by the
Supreme Commander. Such a development would have marked a distinct failure of the Occupation objective of creating a responsible
representative Japanese government. Consequently, a seriously embarrassing contretemps as between the Japanese government and the
Occupation had to be avoided. In short, the job of the Occupation was
to prod and push the government into becoming responsible. But the
approach must be such that the Japanese were not thrown into a tail-
spin or overburdened beyond their capacity.

As we look back now, it is clear that it was the issue of land reform on which both the Occupation and the new generation of Japanese
statesmen and officials achieved the maturity which has made the
Occupation a success. The lessons learned by the Japanese gave them
the confidence that has resulted in a reasonably stable and democratic
government for the past five years. In the case of land reform, the
exercise of restraint and wisdom by all parties involved was an acute
necessity. A hasty or overly forceful handling of the reform issue by
the Occupation might have caused a repudiation by the tenants themselves of any share in a program which involved them in a seriously
embarrassing conflict within the village. Doubtless, even in such a
situation, a land reform of sorts could have been forced into existence.
But such a program could not have lasted. Its difficult administration
and ultimate failure would have afforded an opportunity for totalitarian
propaganda to discredit the Occupation and foment disorder.

Like a good strategist, believing the soundness of his policy was its own best weapon, General MacArthur chose the arena of public opinion as the maneuver ground for testing the acceptability of his agrarian plans. The headquarters staff explained in detail to the Japanese authorities the deficiencies of their law. Occupation specialists demonstrated in practical situations the certain failure of the Japanese law to meet requirements. It was part of Occupation tactics to let informal discussions between lower echelons of both the Japanese government and of the Occupation serve as a means for communicating respective viewpoints. The top Japanese leaders were fully informed by such discussions of the precise particulars by which their law fell short of meeting the Land Reform Directive.

Basic Problems of Land Reform

Still, in spite of their knowledge of these opinions, the Japanese formally presented on March 15, 1946, as their proposals for meeting the Occupation directive, a program which for the most part was based on their December, 1945, law. Perhaps they expected a drastic reaction or an explosion of offended dignity. There is reason to believe that a reaction of this kind would have been a relief, possibly because such an outburst would have entailed a loss of face to the Occupation. In any event, the Japanese officials were disappointed. No sign of dissatisfaction escaped the Headquarters. Instead, the matter was quietly referred back to the Occupation specialists and the long patient course of discussions was renewed.

The essential differences between Japanese and Occupation views on land were simple to state; the implications of these differences were more complex. The Occupation wanted to abolish tenancy promptly. The Japanese proposals were much more moderate. They wished to reform the landlords and permit a considerable amount of tenancy to remain. In their plan, the process of land transfer from landlords to tenants would have been very gradual. They would have permitted landlords at the village level to play a dominant role in determining the land to be transferred to tenants. In other words, the transfer would have been made without disturbing the feudal structure of rural society. From the standpoint of Occupation objectives it was desirable to have tenants assume considerable responsibility in effecting the transfer.

More specifically it was the Occupation's firm intent to bring land ownership status to as many as possible of the more than four million farm families who cultivated wholly or partly land which they did not own. A considerable number of these farmers owned a little portion of the land they farmed but more than one and a half million of them were landless. Thus any approach to complete abolition of tenancy – in other words, any approach to a social and economic change of wide significance – necessitated transfer of ownership of a very large amount of land. A big fraction of the seven million acres of farm land farmed by tenants had to change hands if tenants were to become landowners.

However, these lands represented a principal source of income to a whole class of rent receivers. Many landlords had come to depend on this highly profitable form of investment as a principal means of support. Consequently, such a transfer was bound to be extremely painful to this large group of rentiers. But it should be recalled also that the significance of landlord ownership lay in the benefit to him of a harvest which could be assured only through the toil of some tenant. Thus the economics of land investment for landlords entailed a close-working control of the life and labor of tenants. So the proposed reform signified not only a large transfer of land but also a complete reorientation of the cultivator's motivation.

It was perhaps just as well that the Occupation personnel were able to take a detached view of the impact of their proposals. Apparently the Japanese officials were considerably affected by it. They knew and sympathized with the feelings of the landlord group perhaps more than with the tenants. They realized that deprivation of the handsome profits of tenant operations and of the tremendous social distinction attached to the landlord status could not be achieved painlessly. They were sensitive to social and cultural shocks which the contemplated shift in ownership would cause in the tight village hierarchy.

The rationalization of attitude by Japanese politicians, statesmen, and government administrators was interesting. They seem to have felt that somehow the purpose of the Occupation vis-à-vis tenancy had a moral objective. They conceived that this purpose was really to punish landlordism. This led them to confuse the democratic aims of the reform with the purposes of socialism. In this oversimplified interpretation they assumed that since the Occupation regarded landlordism as bad, then they must view landlords as bad people. From this standpoint they appear to have concluded that the degree of badness was derived from the size of the holding. Thus bigger landlords were more culpable than smaller. This kind of thinking caused them to derive a land reform policy which had a predominant soak-the-rich overtone. Owners of more than 12.25 acres in their law were to be forced to dispose of their holdings while owners of less than that amount went scot free.

From the Occupation viewpoint two things were wrong with this proposal. First, the conversion of the program into an attack on wealth with its class conflict implications was a perversion and a distortion of the central purpose of stabilizing and democratizing the agrarian structure. Second, such an approach made only about 3.3 million acres available for transfer to tenants while 49 per cent of the rented land remained in tenancy.

The Japanese position was, of course, a misconception of the real purpose of the reform. It was necessary to repeat over and over that the objective was to abolish tenancy, not to punish property owners who happened to be landlords. Occupation specialists went into the countryside making studies of actual situations to determine the effect of the Japanese proposals if applied. In several villages where tenancy rates were high, these tests made it plain that the proposals would have had no effect at all, since all landlords owned less than the proposed Japanese limit of 12.25 acres.

Other aspects of these proposals were also unsatisfactory: (1) Too wide a discretion was given local and prefectural agencies of administration, especially when these agencies were heavily weighted with and partial to landlord interests. (2) Landlords could be compelled to sell land only after a complex, lengthy procedure. (3) The program was not easily accessible and comprehensible to tenants who were, for this and other reasons already described, at a great disadvantage vis-à-vis the landlords. (4) The program as designed did not lend itself to effective prompt execution, but facilitated delay and evasion. (5) The legislation made no provision against excessive rents nor for the security of tenure of those who might remain as tenants.

In accordance with General MacArthur's determination to give the whole matter a thorough public airing, land reform was placed as an item on the agenda of the Allied Council for Japan. This advisory body to the Supreme Commander was composed of the Chiefs of Mission of the Allied Powers. It included a representative of the British Commonwealth, the U.S.S.R., China, and the United States. It held regular meetings and announced in advance the agenda for each meeting. Its discussions included many important topics of Occupation policy and the sessions were open to the Allied and United Nations press representatives. These published statements of the press could be republished in Japanese newspapers.

The Council provided a valuable forum and sounding board for raising land reform as a topic for general public debate. Since the group had occasion to devote a considerable amount of time in April, May, and June, 1946, to an open debate of this question, the corresponding period of public consideration was also protracted. In accordance with the anticipations of General MacArthur, the discussion "caught on." By newspaper and radio the debate was carried to every corner of the country. Its effect, as a public issue, was heightened by the simultaneous preparation for the first postwar general elections, foreshadowing a shift in government policies and attitudes.

The Supreme Commander by a directive of January 4, 1946, had disqualified a number of the members of the Shidehara government, cabinet officers and Diet members alike, from the right to hold public office. This action was due to the membership of these individuals in the infamous Imperial Rule Assistance Political Association and similar organizations which had worked for the establishment of a totalitarian, militaristic Japan and complete axis collaboration. In the ensuing elections of April, 1946, the Shidehara government was defeated. It resigned, to be followed by a new government headed by Shigeru Yoshida which was installed on May 1st.

Beginnings of Allied-Japanese Cooperation

Most significant for land reform was the appointment of Hiroo
Wada as Minister of Agriculture and Forestry. Mr. Wada was a dis-
tinctly new type of Japanese statesman. A stocky, vigorous man of
progressive views, he wanted to get things done. He expected his
colleagues and assistants to move forward rapidly in the reconstruction of Japan. Moreover, he recognized that the gap in the views on
land reform between his government and the Occupation would have to
be closed. Therefore he moved expeditiously to resolve the differences.
Some Occupation personnel will long remember the hilarity caused by
the amazing attempts of the interpreters to render into English Mr.
Wada's announcement of his firm intention to see that the Japanese
government "got off the dime" on land reform. Alas! Japanese is far
to formal a language to lend itself to the informal ease of American
slang! Yet the incident seemed to epitomize the new vigorously constructive attitude toward the tangled web of the land reform question.
Pettifogging and maneuvering ceased. Negotiations took a constructive
turn.

Mr. Wada accepted in principle the philosophy of General Mac-
Arthur's directive. As a practical statesman and politician, his problem was to work out a legislative framework whose passage in the
Diet could be obtained. It was also necessary that the program be
administratively feasible within the limitations of Japanese bureaucracy and resources. Fortunately, Wada's course was made progres-
sively easier by the growing success of General MacArthur's strategy
of publicity and debate. The tone of the general election itself had
made it clear that land reform in the Occupation pattern was politically
acceptable. Discussions in the Allied Council were enlightening too,
because they clearly indicated a world attitude of disapproval of the
existing land tenure system and an endorsement of the general pattern
of reform outlined by the Occupation.

In June, 1946, the Allied Council published its conclusions on the
land question. Boiled down, these recommendations approved General
MacArthur's directive and disapproved the plan presented by the
Japanese. The Council further stated its opinion that no one farmer
should be allowed to own over 7.5 acres unless it could be shown that
he had sufficient family labor to cultivate a larger amount or unless a
reduction in acreage would result in lowered production. Any excess
over the legal limit would be purchased by the state together with all
lands owned by absentee landlords. These lands after passing to the
state by virtue of its purchase would then be sold to the tenants. No
negotiations between landlords and tenants would occur except in the
case of a residual amount of rented land. In that case the tenure
would be subject to an obligatory written lease establishing the rights
of the tenant. The actual transfer of land and the accomplishment of
the program would take two years.

In view of these recommendations Mr. Wada had a perfectly clear proposal to consider. His immediate principal concern was to decide whether this program could reasonably be accomplished. There was no obligation for further support of the Shidehara law of December 1945 since the Yoshida government could disclaim all responsibility for it in view of the election. Finally, the only important issue which remained to negotiate was the limit to be set on ownership. The Japanese felt that 7.5 acres was too small in some areas. Yet they recognized the reform could not be effectively carried out with the limit they had set at 12.25 acres if this limit were applied uniformly. An acceptable compromise was effected by setting an over-all standard at 7.5 acres while permitting variations to conform to regional management practices.

Generally this meant that in the areas of northern Honshu where farms were larger, some excess over 7.5 acres would be allowed. On the southerly portions of Honshu and the islands of Kyushu and Shikoku where farms were smaller, rates considerably under 7.5 acres would be set. The northern island of Hokkaido, with an extensive type of agriculture quite different from that in the rest of Japan, was to be treated separately. Farms on that island would be permitted to retain up to 25 acres. With Occupation acceptance of this proposal the only important difference between the two positions was removed.

Matters now moved rapidly. Under Mr. Wada's prodding, numerous ivory-tower Japanese bureaucrats "got off the dime" with the result that on July 26, 1946, the land reform legislation program was handed to the cabinet by Mr. Wada. It contained in addition to the items discussed above some additional provisions:

> Plans for purchase and sale of lands subject to transfer would be determined at the village level by local agricultural land commissions which would have sufficient tenant representatives to protect tenant interests.

> Tenants who had been evicted or were threatened with eviction by landlords in the interval since commencement of legislative consideration of land reform were to receive retroactive protection.

Publication of Wada's program signified the successful conclusion of the negotiations. On August 14, General MacArthur announced publicly his approval of the plan. In September the Japanese government announced its plans for financing the reform program. It calculated that the cost of purchasing land would be ¥12,800,000,000. It was estimated that purchasers would be able to pay in cash only about 30 per cent of the purchase price. It was proposed to finance the balance with bonds issued to the original owners in the amount of 70 per cent of the purchase price.

The long, trying period of discussion and dispute was over. With its passing, a whole new set of duties descended on the agricultural group in the Headquarters. These responsibilities took definite shape with the appearance on August 2 of the English translation of the first draft of the proposed legislation. This document required close scrutiny and study, an extraordinarily tedious and exacting task. Japanese is at best a difficult language. Its vagueness does not disappear in translation to another language. Fluent translation from Japanese to English requires a high degree of scholarship plus a profound knowledge of both languages. Few Europeans and very few Americans possess this skill, and at the time many of the abler Japanese translators had been disqualified by the Occupation purge from handling government work. Consequently the English rendering of the Japanese legislation was something less than a finished literary effort. So the translations on which the Occupation had to work were very rough, requiring both labor and patience to comprehend.

Yet another complication arose from the need to knit the new legislation into the whole structure of Japanese law and particularly into those portions of it concerned with land rights, real property, and agriculture. Some of these antecedent statutes were the outgrowth of centuries of codification and adjudication. Hence it was decided by the Japanese to fix in existing statutes a number of the points in the new land reform policy by the device of amendment. Thus a minimum of new statutes would be required and the new law would gain prestige from its embodiment in older law.

In order to comprehend the proposed legislation, however, it was necessary to study the existing statutes in their entirety and then to re-examine them in the light of the new amendments. Ultimately the vehicle chosen was a series of amendments to The Agricultural Land Adjustment Law of 1938, which were tied by reference to a new statute, The Owner Farmer Establishment and Special Measure Law. In the old statute were placed all principles and standards for tenure relations in agriculture, while the owner-farmer law defined the powers of government to purchase and sell land as well as to designate the land to be transferred.

After days and nights of plowing through the complexities of poorly translated Japanese legal language, Occupation personnel felt they were justified in approving the drafts which were then enacted and promulgated by the Emperor on October 21, 1946. The sigh of relief which accompanied this achievement was offset by the discovery that Japanese laws are put into operation by means of Ordinances. These are documents fully as complex as the laws, of which, on publication, they become a part. Two ordinances are required for each law, a *cabinet ordinance* and a *Ministerial ordinance*. So the deadly round of review of labyrinthine language in tortured syntax was resumed.

Eventually, however, this onerous task too was complete and the ordinances which set the program in motion were finally all promulgated, the last one on December 28, 1946. Thus the entire year 1946 had passed in negotiation, drafting, and enactment of the land reform program which was thus ready for actual execution at the beginning of 1947.

Chapter 8

THE MEN WHO PLANNED
THE LAND REFORM PROGRAM

THE extensive grounds of the Imperial Palace in Tokyo are bordered by a wide and ancient moat. On the farther side of this relic of the Tokugawa dynasty are the streets and buildings of the metropolis. Beside the long easterly reach of the moat runs a long broad avenue. For more than a mile this broad artery stretches almost in a straight line. On the side opposite the moat still stand all the important modern buildings of downtown Tokyo – or all the remaining buildings. This fortunate circumstance is the result of American efforts to avoid bombing the Imperial Palace and its grounds. Along this stretch of avenue are the former Radio Tokyo, the Imperial Hotel, the Imperial Theatre, all principal landmarks of prewar Tokyo. Here too are situated the great business buildings, The Dai Ichi, The Meiji, and the N.Y.K. These and the buildings immediately adjacent, in the years 1945 to 1950, made up the offices and a number of the living quarters of the Allied Occupation personnel.

One of these, The Mitsubishi Shoji Building, housed the Occupation personnel responsible for planning the Japanese land reform program. A few blocks away in a deplorably dilapidated building were the offices of the Ministry of Agriculture and Forestry *(Norinsho)*, where were located the Japanese opposite numbers of the Occupation agriculturists. In these two offices, land and the problems of land were the constant daily preoccupation and concern of a small group of agricultural specialists.

While the preparation for the tremendous land reform operations afforded elements of drama, challenge, and stimulation to those engaged on it, yet it took place against a forlorn background in an atmosphere largely blended of discomfort and melancholy. The year 1946 had been difficult for everyone in Japan. Among the Japanese it had been a grinding day-to-day struggle on the borders of starvation. Occupation personnel, physically comfortable, had to find stimulation in the challenge of their mission to offset their nostalgia, the barrenness of their surroundings, the dullness of army fare. There were also minor discomforts of cheerless offices, stark billets, and the overwhelming physical burden of their work. At least, to those engaged in the project, the year 1947 promised to Japanese and Americans alike the relief of long deferred action.

Yet there was for the Japanese, anyway, a tremendous emotional drain in the postwar period. One of the great evils of war is the postwar reaction. In war, the tempo at least is rapid and terrific emotional stress provides great stimulation. But the quality of the immediate postwar atmosphere of Japan, anyway, was monotony — dull, grayish sameness. This universal note of sameness in a dingy theme affected everyone. The slight but universal smell of sewer gas, the lack of soap, the poor and frequently interrupted electric lights, the dusty, littered offices whose battered furniture skirted complete collapse, the lack of janitorial service, poor paper, half-broken typewriters, and the almost complete absence of heat in the frigid winters were a constant part of the daily working environment of the Japanese.

Their private lives were even more desolate. Many of them commuted for hours from crowded makeshift tenements hastily erected to house bombed-out populations. Their commuting facilities were indescribably awful. They stood for hours in trains from which all windows had long since been removed and which were crowded past normal human endurance. This ordeal was suffered twice a day by many of the men of the Ministry of Agriculture and Forestry. The trains ran infrequently; consequently, when the burden of work required overtime, it meant that they remained all night in the office sleeping on the floor or perhaps on top of a desk.

Occupation personnel were better off, yet the universal disorder and semidiscomfort formed a background against which they lived and worked. If they had some measure of personal comfort, they were aware of the utter shabbiness, hunger, and chronic ill health of their Japanese colleagues. They came to be all the more sensitive because of awareness of the importance of cleanliness, neatness, and order in the Japanese character. Day after day, one gazed out of office windows on half and wholly wrecked buildings, burned homes, and mountains upon mountains of the rubble of destruction. After all, when one's home in the States by contrast seemed so far removed, so bright, so clean, and so happy, was the effort of remaining in Japan worth while? So it required some fortitude, some qualities of imagination, a good deal of conviction in the worthwhileness of land reform to face up to the personal demands which the program presented. Above all perhaps, was the foreboding sense of the magnitude of the undertaking, the sense of a lack of landmarks and guides, and perhaps of the uncertainty of the outcome.

For there is no such thing as a trained land reform personnel. True, individuals may be trained in land economics and in land tenure. One may study the agrarian economy, rural society, and the agricultural policies of nations. There is plenty of material available for the details for carrying out programs of technical guidance in agricultural matters. But the reform of an entire land tenure system in a major nation is a rare event. Consequently, professional preparation for it is impossible. Perhaps only once in an individual's lifetime may there be opportunity to participate in such work.

So the people in Japan who undertook this extraordinary adventure

were mostly people with some knowledge of agriculture, some training perhaps in one or another of its specialized fields, and possessing
some knowledge of government administration. In the main, the more
important job requirement was to be available in the right place –
Japan – at the right time. Most of the Occupation personnel had never
before the war entertained more than the vaguest notions about Japan
and the Japanese. It was chance and the fortunes of war which were
initially responsible for the presence of many of them on the scene.
No one of them had the slightest pretensions to a knowledge of international negotiations or ambitions toward diplomatic careers. Yet
there was something in their common American heritage and personalities which responded to the challenge, a challenge which they met
well in spite of obstacles and handicaps.

The American Personnel

A good deal of the groundwork and many of the basic recommendations for the reform were worked out in the headquarters by men of a
nonmilitary turn of mind. The opinions of these civilian technicians,
in and out of uniform, in a basically military general headquarters
therefore lacked basic authenticity and finality, in the eyes of the staff
of professional soldiers who naturally dominated the Headquarters.
Without the continued firm backing of the Supreme Commander, the
task of the specialists would have been almost impossible, if for nothing else than the lack of mutual understanding with the military. The
offsetting factor therefore was the weight of the personal responsibility of MacArthur. This personal factor had to serve as the main
carrier channel through which decision and action were implemented.
The prompt forthright nature of these decisions and the continued
firm confidence in the work of the agricultural technicians was a
source of encouragement to them and this alone was indispensable to
the success of the project.

Among the civilian professionals, in and out of uniform, the Chief
of the Natural Resources Section of the headquarters, Lt. Colonel
Hubert G. Schenck was responsible for coordination of all activities
affecting natural resources throughout Japan. He had the official duty
of presenting and interpreting the work of the agricultural specialists
to the headquarters staff. A quiet, unassuming professor of geology
and an outstanding American scientist accustomed to the placid functions of teaching and research, Colonel Schenck made the transition
to an extraordinarily complex assignment in Japan with considerable
success. He soon found the task of fitting a group of scientists and
technicians into the rigid framework of a military headquarters was
no simple matter. Moreover the art of developing among professional
military men respect for the judgments and opinions of scientists and
technicians was a wearing task of diplomacy. The Colonel ran interference for a wide assortment of technicians and scientists. At the
same time, he held together in an organizational framework a wide
variety of highly individualistic personalities and temperaments.

The fortunes of war, the element of chance, and the vicissitudes of government administration had thrown all these different people together in a haphazard fashion under Colonel Schenck's supervision. In ordinary circumstances of civilian administration, men work together for months and even for years developing an intimate knowledge of each other's capacities and deficiencies. This association constitutes an invaluable aid to a smoothly running organization. In the circumstances of the Occupation, men arrived overnight to fill unexpected vacancies caused by illness, expired contracts, family troubles at home, or expiration of time limits for overseas duty. So this graying Stanford professor carried on a successful undertaking by dint of almost daily invention and improvisation out of a vigorous resourcefulness which perhaps would have amazed former pupils in the Palo Alto classrooms.

Among the Colonel's principal associates was Dr. Leonard, a leading American agronomist. Dr. Leonard's academic career at Colorado A. and M. College had been interrupted by a call to military duty early in the war. So this agricultural scientist found himself in a variety of roles as diplomat, legal analyst, and administrator, all in the course, perhaps, of a single day's work. Following Leonard was Raymond Davis, an able administrator originally of the Soil Conservation Service. Perhaps Wolf Ladejinsky from the Department of Agriculture's Office of Foreign Agricultural Relations knew more as a student about the general topic of land reform in its historical, political, and economic aspects than anyone else. His tremendous enthusiasm for the Japanese program was a continuous energizing factor in its accomplishment. Ladejinsky was the brilliant, indefatigable salesman of ideas about land tenure. His enthusiasm brooked no obstacles. Not even the sacred precincts of high military rank prevented his carrying the gospel directly to the fountain head of all authority.

Ladejinsky's close associate was Gilmartin, a captain, yanked into the army before the ink on his Ph.D. at California was dry. Gilmartin's excellent academic training served him well as a careful analyst of Japanese agricultural problems and its rural economy. With a ceaseless, steady, penetrating drive he and Ladejinsky pushed through the smoke screens of landlord politics finally to crystallize the Occupation position on land reform. But it was Robert S. Hardie, a former artillery captain, originally from Nebraska, with a fund of experience on the social problems of agriculture, particularly among the agricultural migrants of California, who set the terrific pace of work which finally got the program in motion. His tremendous physical endurance and drive pushed through a daily output that taxed everyone around him and forced many of the Japanese to the point of exhaustion. This contribution was essential in the face of all sorts of shortages both in material and personnel. Invaluable aid came from Takahashi, formerly a graduate student from the University of Chicago, later a soldier in the Occupation forces. Though Takahashi read and spoke

Japanese, his chief contribution was a smooth-running, tireless intellect which solved with ease so many of the incredible daily administrative puzzles which the Japanese have a genius for manufacturing. There was Dorothy Goodwin from Connecticut, who had lived at one time in India. Finally, the writer of this narrative, from California, with a background of government work in the Department of Agriculture, who had specific responsibility for executing the land reform program plan as it was finally formulated on January 1, 1947.

There we were, thousands of miles from our various home states, of diverse backgrounds, with different training, yet all working together to bring into reality a new agrarian structure for Japan. We learned as we worked. But first of all we had to learn to work with the Japanese. For it was not easy to establish effective working relations, either for the Occupation personnel or for the Japanese in the stiff formality of a victor-vanquished framework reinforced by the strait jacket of non-fraternization. Americans work hard but they are at their most efficient in easy relations with their fellow workers, and despite relative official status, the Japanese agricultural specialists were, in fact, fellow workers.

The Japanese Personnel

At first there was mutual distrust. While the Japanese are by no means a fearful people, it could not have been very pleasant to deal face to face with men who for the time being represented almost absolute power and who might very well bear profound animosity. It must have taken some little courage even to enter the heavily guarded Occupation offices under the cold, watchful stares of well-armed Military Policemen. Moreover, many of the Occupation personnel had come up the long and bitter journey "through the islands," as soldiers. For these men it was difficult to maintain a dispassionate bearing toward representatives of what had so recently been a ferocious and hated enemy. For the rest of us there was perhaps some of the inevitable peculiar slant of Americans, no matter how consciously unprejudiced and otherwise sophisticated, toward all foreigners and particularly those of a different race. Principally this attitude seems to be a mixture of naive condescension and doubt. The self-control of the meticulous Japanese must have been sorely tried by many of our early attitudes and behaviors.

On the other hand, Japanese initial insistence on protocol and long, stiff preambles seemed to us to take up inordinate amounts of good productive working time. Then, too, the long fencing bout over basic principles of the reform was a terribly trying period for both groups. Elaborate involutions of oriental argumentation in favor of *their* proposals confronted the blunt stubborn endurance of the Americans. These tactics rubbed on each other hourly, daily, weekly for month after month.

But to both groups this period served to prove as nothing else can prove that men who work hard together, even though in disagreement, cannot remain hostile indefinitely. Despite protocol, non-fraterniza- tion, and relative official position personalities will emerge — this one is witty, that one patient and wise, another is stupid, while still an- other is just tired and ill. One becomes aware of names and matches them with faces to which are related stature, traits, and gestures. So, finally, there is after all, not a Japanese official nor an American bu- reaucrat, but a man rather more than less intelligent who is trying to do his job.

Wada, the Minister and later a sort of middle-aged elder statesman, created always an atmosphere of cheerfulness and confidence. "Yes," he seemed to say, "it *is* a difficult problem and the odds are against us, but a solution must be found and somehow I will find it." He al- ways did. In one top level conference on an extremely important matter, the spokesman for the Occupation ended by saying that now, the Japanese, having heard the Occupation viewpoint, might retire and think the matter over for a few days and present a reply reflecting their unified opinion. Mr. Wada, without a moment's hesitation re- plied that time was precious to the Japanese as to the Occupation and he saw no need to use it for a purely ceremonial purpose since he already knew what the answer would be. Without waiting for a reply he went on to outline their position briefly and lucidly. Forthwith, in their presence, he mentioned by name men in his group who would at first be opposed, pointed out their mistaken position and its futility. "Mr. So-and-so has doubts about this statement because he thinks it means such-and-such an outcome. However, he has neglected to con- sider this or that point, so he will in the end be convinced." It was a tour de force both of character and of reason! One couldn't help thinking at the time of our misconceptions about the "devious and in- direct Japanese," for here was directness and frankness with a venge- ance.

Not infrequently discussions between American and Japanese officials became tremendously involved, so involved that both sides thankfully retired for reflection and reinforcement. Sometimes these engagements reached a deadlock. The Japanese thought we were wrong and said so — on the whole more politely than we in imparting similar information to them. On such occasions the Japanese often called in Mr. Saseyama. Perhaps he should be called "Saseyama the Peacemaker." As Vice Minister of Agriculture, he had, next to Mr. Wada, principal authority in that ministry. His role as mediator be- came so well known that occasionally in heated discussion someone would suggest that it was about time to call in Mr. Saseyama!

A quiet, grave, and reflective person, he gave thoughtful attention to the statement of an Occupation argument and somehow a wise com- promise seemed to come to him. His face was broad and a little heavy, with an expression of a mingled sadness and kindliness. Humor, which he sometimes permitted himself to display, was gentle and com- passionate. It was necessary once or twice to discuss with him the

well-established incompetence of one of his officials. On one such
occasion he sadly remarked that, since the man worked for him, he
probably knew far more about his incompetence than we did. He continued that he always had hopes of improvement in these cases, for it
seemed to him that the more incompetent a man was the greater the
possibility for improvement!

Then there was Mr. Yamazoe, whose casual attitude and apparent
indifference were the manifestations of a cool incisive intellect. His
gray head was closely cropped in the Buddhist fashion. Although not
young, his face was smooth, unlined, and boyishly good-looking. This
official's characteristic half smile, closed eyes, and negligent attitude
in the rising temperature of acrimonious debate sometimes acted as a
goad to western tempers and temperaments. One suspected that Mr.
Yamazoe was perfectly conscious that his demeanor was irritating to
people weary from long hours of stubborn resistance, oppressed and
wretched with monsoon season humidity and prickly heat. For long
periods, as arguments waxed furiously, this polished gentleman sat
with closed eyes, immobile, detached, wordless. Yet when he finally
spoke it was to dominate the group by virtue of his intense concentration on and mastery of the subject.

Eldest of the group was Dr. Tanabe, older and it sometimes seemed,
wearier. A man of slight physical stature but a veteran of years of
fruitless fighting for tenure reform, Dr. Tanabe was perhaps better
informed on the technical aspects of agriculture than his colleagues,
possibly a more scholarly man than in either group. But it was his
long stubborn work in behalf of the tenants which entitled him to
respect. In our country, a fighter for a cause, however hopeless,
usually has some kind of a following to cheer him on and to restore
his confidence in the hours of defeat. But the Japanese deliberately
use the weapon of ostracism as a means of punishment to coerce the
man with unacceptable ideas. So in the long years of Dr. Tanabe's
struggle his only ally was a sense of right based on careful study.
Arrayed on the other side was all that stood for power, for correct-
ness as a Japanese, for social recognition, and for professional ad-
vancement. To such a man, professional life meant complete isolation
in a scholastic backwater. Students hesitated to associate themselves
with his beliefs. Colleagues pitied or hated him. Over all was a constant threat of outright suppression, imprisonment, loss of employment, and economic sanctions.

Men who will face up to this kind of persecution are rare. They
are lonely men to whom advancing years frequently bring no reward.
Yet over the world there are many such. In their unheard, unseen
steadfastness and stubborn devotion lies a great reservoir of strength
in the battle for freedom. These men must be sought out, for their
virtues do not shine in the front rank of the illustrious. It was Dr.
Tanabe's fortune to find himself vindicated and his position accepted
within the span of his working life. He was a lucky exception, for
many such as he must leave the scene with no sense of accomplishment.

The discipline which life had wrought on the older men, Saseyama, Yamazoe, and Tanabe, gave them strength and marked character, but all in the framework of Japanese life and manners. For them the adjustment to working and thinking as part of an international group was more difficult than among the younger Japanese in the Ministry of Agriculture. Fortunately these youngsters had to carry many day-to-day details of the work. Always loyal to their superiors, to their country's welfare, they were, nevertheless, in those splendid learning years when the mind is still fresh and the capacity of the intellect still unexplored. Despite the disaster of the war, a good deal of personal tragedy, and much hardship, the Occupation was after all a great adventure for them. From somewhere, they found strength to meet the terrific demands on energy to carry an amazing amount of work. They responded with enthusiasm to the opportunity to engage in the great reform. As one of them put it, "Our zeal for agricultural reform made possible great sacrifices and a pure unselfishness."

They endowed these foreigners, perhaps as any young person might, with qualities of romance, with the adventure of far places, and of attractiveness far beyond reality. Whatever of skill or information the Americans might display, they intended somehow to seize, to explore, and win for themselves. Thus the flexibility of American thinking and its empirical instrumentalist approach provided new horizons to these young products of the rigors of Tokyo Imperial University College of Law. Of these men there were three particularly who worked with the headquarters agricultural specialists in what finally became a team. These were T. Iwozumi, H. Tokoro, and K. Owada.

Tokoro had responsibility for the land use and reclamation aspects of the work. Owada toiled over administrative and legislative problems of land reform assisted by the economics and statistics which Iwozumi provided. During the first months of 1945 all three loyally supported the "first land reform" provided by the Japanese law of December, 1945. After all, they had had a hand in designing it and to some extent felt it was *their* law. Almost daily they trudged into the Mitsubishi Shoji Building laden with voluminous documents carried in their *furoshiki* – large silk scarves which are tied cornerwise around the contents. Their confidence in and respect for the written word was enormous. Their pockets and their minds literally bulged with this kind of proof.

Of course, both sides suffered from the great handicap of language. So both Owada and Tokoro, as part of what they conceived to be their responsibility, found time somewhere to improve their English to the point of being able to carry on a satisfactory conversation. All three could read it. By the time the final legislation of 1946, The Land Reform Law, had become a fact in late 1946, all three had fitted into a workable pattern with the Occupation personnel. They had come to know each other's ways, weaknesses, and strength and were able to communicate with one another in practical ease.

Tokoro had a lively and gracious sense of humor. His courtesy and gentleness were underlain with characteristic Japanese firmness

and even stubbornness. Time after time he imperturbably bundled up
his numerous papers and went off, in what seemed conclusive defeat,
only to reappear again after a day or so to reopen the whole matter
with a charming disregard for the fact that in our minds the matter
had been completely and irrevocably settled. Occupation personnel
after a few experiences with Tokoro-san looked into the future with
misgivings, visualizing perhaps in the months and years ahead an
eternally reappearing Tokoro, never defeated in spite of resounding
arguments or forcefully expressed commands.

Owada, with an excellent background of economic training, used a
powerful mind and inexhaustible energy to drive through, past, and
over the many obstacles to a practical reform program. His strength
seemed to lie in his ability to synthesize desirable economic and
social objectives with practical political and legal means for achiev-
ing them. His ingenuity in this respect far outstripped the capacity of
many of the Occupation people. His voluminous written production,
which, originally rendered in Japanese, had to be translated by him
into English, meant late hours for his Occupation opposite numbers.
Beneath this driving capacity for work was a profound emotional motivation for the improvement of the condition of the Japanese peasant,
mixed with a mystical appreciation for the good, the true, and the
beautiful in Japan and in Japanese life.

Being a sensitive man, Owada understood quickly the basic good
will and ethical intentions of the Occupation personnel. He saw earlier
than most the real value for his people inherent in the Occupation objectives. At times he seemed to glow with the realization of what it
all could mean. Despite the seriousness of his purpose, there was
about Owada an enthusiasm, almost a breathless eagerness that was
truly charming. Once he said, almost rapturously, during a favorable
major turn in events, "We are like the French Revolution or the
American Revolution – but more like the French Revolution." In
retrospect it seems now that among the Japanese Owada must take a
great deal of the credit and responsibility for the Japanese Land Reform. One hopes that this recognition will actually be accorded – it
is a matter, unfortunately, not without doubt. Owada was not popular
with the old guard Japanese leaders.

Once, at one of the rare social gatherings of Japanese celebrities
and top Occupation "brass," several Japanese notables allowed themselves to be formally introduced to Mr. Owada by his Occupation colleagues. Again, while visiting a former Japanese nobleman of the old
regime, we discussed the problems of agrarian Japan. The old man
had been a member of the House of Peers in the pre-surrender days,
and had attended the same New England college from which I had
graduated. Supposedly he was a man of affairs. Yet when I remarked
that Mr. Owada was one of the important younger men in the public
life of Japan, he replied, "I never heard of him." Perhaps in this attitude lies part of the meaning of the agrarian reform – the old leadership of Japan, custom-ridden and dying, in contrast with the Japan
represented by the vitality, vigor, and enthusiasm of men like Owada.

Chapter 9

DEVELOPMENT OF A GRASS ROOTS
REFORM ORGANIZATION

THE reformation of a nation's land tenure system must rest on a sound foundation of law and policy. But above all, it must be carefully planned. Then, it must have an adequate structure of organization to carry out the planning. Laws, policy, and plans cannot be created overnight, but in their essential development they do not involve many people. Even so, they are only a start. But finally a large and widespread organization, comprehending many skills and diverse functions, to carry out the work once the legal and planning phases have been achieved, must be created. This organization must be trained and disciplined for the specific functions it is to perform. A democratically oriented tenure reform program, within a policy framework which respects property rights, must be large enough to handle in detail each individual property transfer. It is obvious that such a program utilizes the services of many more people than are required in revolutionary or totalitarian schemes, whose principal objective is simply to turn out one set of land occupiers in favor of another set. Yet, as the number of workers increase and the operating criteria become more refined, the tasks of administration become increasingly heavy.

So the small group of Japanese government and Allied Occupation planners were faced, in the closing weeks of 1946, with the formidable task of mobilizing and training a very large administrative force. This organization had to be capable of executing the reform program in each of Japan's 46 major political subdivisions. These prefectures, or *ken,* contained over 11,000 cities, towns, and villages. These communities constituted the basic political subdivisions of which rural Japan is composed. Since some of Tokyo planners were well experienced in the art of government administration, they recognized that the work must be achieved within the existing framework of established organization both in the Japanese government and in the Occupation. This objective could be realized by expanding existing administrative structures, by shifting the emphasis of established functions, and by grafting new functions onto older ones. Initially, of course, it is faster and easier to create new organizations outside the existing framework, and also it is much more fun. But, when permanent long-term goals are sought, it is wiser to work within the existing structure. In this

74

way all the contributing services and experience of trained personnel in the regular establishment of government are focused on the central task without disruption. Then too, it is much less expensive to work within the established framework.

Principal among existing organizations capable of serving the Japanese side of the work was the Agricultural Land Department of the Ministry of Agriculture and Forestry at Tokyo, with its eight strategically located regional offices. Next were the agricultural departments of the prefectural governments which were accustomed to very close working relations with the Regional Land Offices. Through these regional establishments the *ken* agricultural departments were tied into central policy and central government control. Prefectural departments carried on their work through smaller administrative units known as *gun,* somewhat like our counties minus their political independence. The prefectural government machinery at the *gun* level dealt with the affairs of the local villages within the *gun* through the channels of village government.

On the Occupation side all policy making and general guidance functions were vested in General MacArthur and his headquarters in Tokyo. The actual administration and enforcement of Occupation policy, however, was a responsibility of the Eighth United States Army, which was directly responsible for administering civilian affairs throughout Japan. These civil affairs responsibilities were primarily those of observation, surveillance, and reporting.

Eighth Army carried out these functions primarily through military government "teams" (later called Civil Affairs Teams) composed of specialists in various categories of government, law, agriculture, and economics. These teams were located at the principal city of each of the prefectures. Thus it was the Agricultural Officer, frequently a civilian, of the military government team who was to safeguard the proper functioning of the land reform program at the prefectural and *gun* level. He would supervise the program among the multitude of cities, towns, and villages of the prefectures.

A great deal of the credit for the successful functioning of the Occupation of Japan is due to the men of these military government teams. More often than not the teams were understaffed. Frequently they were remote from other Occupation units. Communications were poor and at times nonexistent. Thus in many instances a handful of Americans, surrounded by millions of Japanese, represented, in distant and sometimes inaccessible districts the core of the Occupation policy. It was their duty, in spite of language difficulties, unfamiliarity with local political complexities, evasion, poor communications, lack of adequate services and equipment, to insure full compliance with the Land Reform Law. Their only really effective weapon of enforcement was their own confidence and the respect which they as individuals were able to command among the Japanese.

Personnel of the teams were of all sorts and kinds with different backgrounds of education and experience. But, shocking to sticklers

for specialized academic training and to those who demand specific
experience as essentials to job placement, there seemed to be no significant correlation between their backgrounds and the success or
failure of these military government officers. A youngster who had
graduated from an agriculture course at a state university did well.
But so also did a former Chicago night club manager, matured in the
flames of Leyte, Okinawa, and Iwo Jima. On inspection trips from
Tokyo one was met by newly assigned agricultural officers at lonely
stations who anxiously confided that only ten days before they had commanded a rifle company.

Sometimes, the regularly assigned officer had returned to the
States. In the interval before his replacement arrived the burden of
responsibility descended on a non-commissioned officer. Sergeants
and corporals, seasoned by experience with Stilwell in the China
theatre, or perhaps by years in a Japanese prison camp, met and
mastered innumerable problems and technical details. Their only
resource for meeting the new responsibility, aside from military
training, was sheer nerve and typical American ingenuity. Perhaps
the task would have been easier if there had been available more men
with proper training and education. But it seemed that men with such
qualifications preferred their regular work at home and the uninter-
rupted pursuit of their careers in familiar surroundings. So there
was no choice but, as the army puts it, to do it "the hard way" – and
for the most part it was done extremely well.

In the prefectures as in Tokyo a trend toward integration of effort
between Japanese and Americans arising from the compulsion of the
job gradually broke down the barriers of speech, custom, and relative
official status. In most prefectures this integration did not approach
the common understanding achieved in Tokyo. Perhaps this was due
sometimes to the presence in the area of politically powerful members
of the landlord group. In some instances these combined to make their
influence felt in prefectural government circles. Indeed, in a few cases
the prefectural government personnel were themselves part of the
landlord coterie. In other prefectures, such as Shiga ken in central
Honshu, the feudal tradition was very strong and the opposition to the
land program bitter. Here widespread distrust and suspicion were
aroused among the citizens against the prefectural officials by rumors
that they were cooperating too closely with the Occupation. In Hiroshima ken, the bitterness of landlord feeling turned to such hatred of
prefectural officials, because of their part in the land reform program,
that many of the latter preferred to resign rather than live under the
strain of the intense local hostility. Yet in time, as the landlord influence waned, these barriers to cooperation were partially overcome, and the two groups of officials came to work together effectively.

Training the Prefectural Administrators

But, before any work at all could be commenced, this diverse group of Occupation and Japanese officials had to be made aware of their responsibilities and duties in the land reform program. In addition, the prefectural government staff had to be greatly expanded. New workers had to be recruited. Fortunately the earlier pre-surrender attempts at land reform had necessitated the training and orientation of a considerable number of junior officials. A number of these men had gained some actual experience in administering those earlier laws before being called into the military service. With demobilization, some of these men became available for the new program. Along with its recruitment program, the Japanese organized at Tokyo a series of training conferences late in 1946 and early in 1947. The conferees were brought into Tokyo from all over Japan. For many this plan entailed long and arduous travel.

Travel conditions for Japanese were very bad. From Kagoshima in southern Kyushu a trip to Tokyo meant at least a 30-hour ride in windowless cars, all terribly overcrowded. The cars were freezingly cold in winter and suffocating in the summer heat. Many travelers had to stand the entire distance. There was no food other than that which the passenger carried with him. There were no washroom facilities and no opportunity for sleep. After such a ride the Japanese official traveler arriving in Tokyo, hungry, tired, and dirty, was confronted by the fact that little could be done to remove these stains of travel. How he was to eat, sleep, and keep clean while in Tokyo were matters of almost complete conjecture. One just had to do the best one could between conference sessions.

The sessions consisted of three or four days of intensive cramming on such topics as (1) explanations of the new law and its contrast with earlier laws, (2) means for providing farmers with information and advice on purchase and sale provisions of the new law, (3) budget and organizational procedures, (4) administrative methods, and (5) conditions in rural areas and possible farmer reactions to the new law. Immediately on adjournment of conferences, the travelers were expected to return in the same fashion whence they came. On arrival at his regular headquarters, after such an ordeal, the prefectural official plunged immediately into development of a training program, similar to the one he had attended in Tokyo, for the benefit of his own staff.

Fortunately several of these conferences had been held in 1946 before the final enactment of the new legislation. Consequently, prefectural staffs had become oriented to some degree in the general features of the new legislation. By January, 1947, there were over 100 key senior officials scattered through the 46 prefectural governments who had received a broad indoctrination and some training in the new program. These intensive training periods for selected senior personnel had also been strengthened by a series of three-day schools for junior officials at the Gotemba Agricultural School in Shizuoka ken.

As a result, over 300 junior workers had been brought in touch with
the new program. Of course the greatest instrument for this training
was simply the human memory. Materials were extremely meager.
They consisted mostly of one copy of the proposed law for each trainee.
Instruction followed the usual lecture and discussion procedure.

Among Occupation personnel the problem of training and orientation was simpler because there were so few to be trained. But in
other respects it was much more difficult. Training required a clear
exposition of the horribly complex language of the law and its affili-
ated ordinances, for these were to be the authoritative guide which
must be followed precisely. Introduction to the formidable complexities of the law in its English form initially brought reactions among
military government personnel ranging from shock to unbelief and
despair. Attempts to brief the law into simpler language were made,
of course, but sometimes this process involved more trouble than it
was worth. Before such a condensation could be published it had to be
checked back through retranslation into Japanese for accuracy — and
it never came out the same! Indeed, comprehension of the law defied
a good many of the normal teaching and study methods. Actually it
was necessary to live through a number of concrete situations before
meaning could be extracted from the jumble of words.

All these conferences and discussions resulted finally in a vast
activity both in the crowded corridors of prefectural capital buildings
and in the starkly furnished quarters of the military government teams.
Team personnel were alerted to their new responsibilities at a three-
day conference, December 11 to 13, 1946. This meeting took place at
the once lovely resort hotel on the beautiful Atami peninsula not far
from Tokyo. General MacArthur officially notified Eighth Army of its
role in the program on January 8, 1947.

There was to be theoretically, at least, in each of the 46 prefectures one Occupation specialist who possessed some knowledge of the
program. Among the Japanese there were scattered through prefectural governments some 400 workers of various grades who had received a fairly specific, though brief, orientation in the work they were
to perform. For both groups there was little time for speculation as
to the ideological or political significance of the program. Its imposing bulk loomed immediately in the foreground. Moreover, the formidable character of the undertaking was reinforced by General Mac-
Arthur's demand for its accomplishment within two years from
January 1, 1947.

Formation of Village Land Commissions

It was a major part of the concepts of the Tokyo planners that a
great share of responsibility for the reform should be borne by the
peasants themselves. They considered that tenure reform, to be effective, should be the outward manifestation of a great process of
rural re-education and social reconstruction. It was essential that

the program, conceived in contexts of economic and political liberalism, seeking emancipation of working farmers from the yoke of serfdom, must be accomplished with a minimum of intervention from Japanese bureaus or from the Occupation. Thus viewed, government became an instrument for assisting and advising farmers. They were to receive help in executing the law and in giving their acts a proper official form, but they were not to be deprived of initiative nor overburdened with bureaucratic details.

For this reason the administrative pattern was deliberately planned so that the initial action would take place in the villages. The dynamic element was therefore the Village Land Commission. The action of these bodies set in motion the whole machinery up through the *gun* and prefectural governments and into the ministry at Tokyo. The whole structure was to receive all its important energizing impulses from actions by the people, thus completely reversing the entire historical trend of relations between the Japanese government and the Japanese people.

This principle of citizen participation was elaborated by other commissions made up of rural people at the prefectural and national level. These prefectural and national commissions paralleled the prefectural and national agencies of government. Prefectural Land Commissions worked directly as a reviewing agency of the Village Land Commission decision. However, approval by the Prefectural Commissions of local commission recommendations constituted an official order on the prefectural government for finalizing the action. Another body of citizens, the Central Agricultural Land Commission, acted as an advisor to the Minister of Agriculture and Forestry.

Since the structure was designed to be set in motion from below, an important item in the business of setting it up was a nationwide election of Village Land Commissioners. But before an election could be held, it was necessary to instruct the rural citizenry in conducting such an election. The first step was to register in each village all tenants, landlords, and owner-farmers in their separate categories. One imagines after the long period of waiting and tension in the villages that the impact of this formal procedure was an excruciating experience – like putting a dentist's drill on an exposed nerve.

For with this action, the die was cast; a tenant was a tenant, officially classified as such and subject to the rights and obligations which the new law established for him. There would be, after registration, no chance for him to seek the comfort of anonymity and ambiguity by voting for or combining with feudal superiors or in making other gestures which would in effect say, "Let's forget the whole thing." Indeed to these humble people, this first freshening breeze of the air of freedom must have seemed a chilly draught indeed. The realization that they *must* be registered as tenants and as tenants *must* vote only for tenant representatives came as a distinct shock. At this point it is quite probable that the entire village would gladly have accepted the hand of the paternal authority and returned to the status quo ante.

Probably with similar reservations, landlords learned that they could
vote only for landlord representatives and owner-farmers were informed that they too would place in nomination only candidates legally
qualified as owner-farmers.

The Commissions were ten-man bodies with five tenant, two owner-
farmer, and three landlord representatives. The distribution of membership was based on the assumption that owner-farmers would generally act in conjunction with landlords, an assumption later found to
be completely accurate. The arrangement originally proposed by the
Japanese government for having equal representation for each category would have meant almost always that tenants would have been in
the minority.

When the villagers realized the full significance of the impending
elections there were many secret caucuses among the folk who had
traditionally held the reins of social control. *Buraku* elders met together and sat late, gravely pondering the situation. Tenants became
exceedingly shy and skittish. They went about the village quietly and
as unobtrusively as possible, perhaps feeling somewhat like over-
grown adolescents at their first party. At least that's how they be-
haved. Landlords adopted a benign and paternal demeanor and paid
their tenants seemingly inr   ent visits whose principal objective was
to call attention to the beauties o. ld Japanese traditions and the
sacredness of feudal obligations. Sometimes they called up poignant
memories of bygone days and of ancestral ties which had held the two
families together over the centuries.

One can imagine that about this time our tenant friend, Joe Tanaka,
was quite unhappy about the whole idea of land reform. Heretofore, in
all public matters he had been accustomed to follow the lead of his
feudal leader who was, in most instances, a landlord. After a matter
had been settled with the landlord or one of his associates safely en-
sconced in office, Joe could hope that out of the goodness of his heart
or from a sense of duty to a feudal inferior, the new incumbent might
see his way to a consideration of some of the Tanaka family's more
pressing problems. But the matter was handled indirectly, obliquely
— always with the implication that it was a personal matter, a favor,
granted by a superior to a petitioner, not a matter of right and law.
In this manner local politics of the Japanese village had customarily
functioned from time immemorial. Opponents in politics were feudal
superiors each with his own following of peasants who were for the
most part his tenants. These leaders then maneuvered their respective followings in the gambits of political strategy.

Now, in a time of crisis, the Joe Tanaka's found themselves unable
to be of any assistance to the traditional superiors. As a tenant they
would automatically, along with other tenants, be forced by the terms
of the law to seek their own candidates. Not easily, in the customary,
well-worn undemocratic way, but making a deliberate choice, painfully
guided only by the dictates of their own intelligence and by discussion
with other tenants. It was a path full of stumblings and missteps.

The landlords, seeing that there was no legal method by which they could use the tenant vote, sought then to influence the selection of tenant commissioners. They calculated on coercing their own tenants into voting for a tenant who would be, in effect, a landlord dummy. If they could achieve success in this, they calculated on gaining working control of the commission.

In quite a number of instances Joe Tanaka fell for this strategy, particularly in the more remote and inaccessible districts. Yet, this game had important weaknesses, principally the psychological one of emphasizing the equality between Joe and the dummy candidate. It seemed to Joe that he had done the landlord a favor in voting for his candidate. But it was inevitable that he should come to see that an unwarranted honor had been conferred on one of his own equals. As the strangeness of the new situation wore off, he came to feel that his representative owed him something. Moreover, it was quite plain that in the eyes of the law this conclusion was correct and could be enforced.

But there was a wide range in the outcome of this situation. People in the areas close to the big metropolitan centers were in some instances more sophisticated and less likely to accept the landlord version of the case. Likewise, they were susceptible to more modern forms of political corruption. In the central Honshu prefecture of Okayama many villages had traditionally been centers of resurgent tenant activity. Here the landlords had no chance whatever of influencing the vote. In the remote mountain villages of Nagano and Niigata, almost completely inaccessible in the winter months, there was a tendency to overlook the matter of the election completely. One entire prefecture on the island of Shikoku and another on the island of Kyushu failed almost completely to recognize the election because the governor was personally opposed to the reform.

Again, it was difficult for the village to escape the traditional *buraku* influence. Perhaps it was too much to expect that many villages could hold an election without a preselection of candidates by the *buraku* family-head councils. Moreover, on close examination there was the problem of loss of face in the *buraku* by a defeated candidate if more than one candidate from the *buraku* stood for election for the same post. On the other hand, rivalry between *buraku* was an accepted custom. Consequently, there was no problem in having the candidate of one *buraku* compete with a candidate from another *buraku*. But *buraku* interference in the election was not a good thing. *Buraku* influences in many ways paralleled traditional controls of feudalism. Preselection by the *buraku* of commission candidates tended therefore to reflect a considerable degree of landlord pressure, even though the majority of the *buraku* families were tenants.

In spite of all these adverse factors, these times of crisis produced some heartening examples of the essential decency found among human beings. This was evidenced in the landlord group itself by some fine and generous men, in widely separated areas, who gave the leadership necessary to push the local reform and to expedite its work.

Perhaps this could happen only in Japan or among oriental people. At
any rate their behavior was splendid and inspiring. In order to remove any doubt of their good faith and to insure their effectiveness,
these men first divested themselves of any interest in land. They
turned over their entire holdings to the village authorities for later
distribution to the tenants. Such men were rare, but their fame was
widespread and their action set a goal of behavior in the tradition of
Buddhist selflessness and of samurai chivalry.

Thus a great many different factors entered into shaping the results of the nationwide election of land commissioners. There were
the selfish machinations of landlords in Oita ken and the outright
intimidation of tenants on Kyushu and in Kochi, on Shikoku. Resurgent peasant sentiment was common near the big cities and in Okayama ken. There were ethical challenges among the landlords which
produced effective leadership for the reform in several districts.
Everywhere was the universal cultural influence of the *buraku* with its
insistence on the family and ancestral codes. A comprehension of the
relative influences of all these factors prevented any anticipation that
the election would be a universal success. It could only be regarded
as a first step which, however fumbling and halting, was an essential
element in creating a sense of self-direction and purpose among the
peasant group.

The election of Village Land Commissions was held throughout
Japan in the latter half of December, 1946. On January 8, 1947, the
Ministry of Agriculture and Forestry reported that nearly 108,000
local commissioners had been elected and 10,770 local commissions
had been established. In about 5,000 localities the number of candidates exactly equaled the number of commissioners to be elected,
with the result that in these communities there had been no election
contest whatever. This outcome raised the question as to whether an
election of any kind had occurred in these places or whether some
other device for the selection of commissioners had not been used.
A careful investigation made through military government channels
revealed that a considerable number of deviations had taken place; yet
the selection of about 75 per cent of the commissions conformed to an
acceptable degree of democratic process. In some 2,900 communities
the results were definitely unacceptable. In six prefectures practically no effort had been made by the authorities to prepare farmers
for the election.

Immediate steps were taken to correct the situation. New carefully supervised elections were held. No punishment was necessary
since the deep sense of disgrace caused by the attendant publicity was
ample punishment for the entire community. The consequent loss of
face to those who had advised such a course, and to their candidates,
was almost overwhelming.

Actually, the uncontrollable factor in most of these cases was not
intentional bad faith, but rather ignorance of any method other than
the ancient *buraku* discussion method of political action. It developed

that what was a fairly representative and democratic choice in one
buraku was the very opposite in another.

These miscarriages ultimately did no great harm. The simple
recall procedure provided by the Land Reform Law was widely pub-
licized with detailed instructions for putting it in effect. Due to this
original emphasis the recall method became one of the standard procedures by which the tenants gradually asserted their growing independence and political awareness. In the winter and early spring of
1947, following the initial election, hundreds of recall elections were
called by the tenants themselves. Out of the first 500 or so of the
voluntarily invoked recall elections all the tenant representatives
were displaced.

Election of Commissioners

Election of the 20-member Prefectural Land Commissions were
held from February 20 to 25, 1947. The village land commissioners
were electors of the prefectural commissioners, and the election was
their first official act. Prefectural Land Commissions had ten tenant
representatives, six landlord representatives, and four representatives of owner-farmers. Each category was elected by the corresponding category of village commissioners.

As we have stated, the functions of the Prefectural Land Commissions were primarily to review and endorse the decisions of the village commissions. Important also was their duty as appeal bodies
hearing arguments and judging the merits of appeals from the decisions of the village commissions. Moreover, Prefectural Land Commissions could remove village commissions which failed to function
and on sufficient evidence of bad faith could themselves undertake the
duties of the local body. Their endorsement of the action with regard
to a piece of land taken by a local commission carried with it a demand for official certification by the prefectural governor as deputy
of the central government of the consummation of that act.

Prefectural Land Commission elections went smoothly, resulting in
the election of 1,150 commissioners. These were divided into 460
tenant representatives, 276 landlord representatives, and 184 owner-
farmer representatives. By law, the prefectural governor was permitted to select and appoint five neutral commissioners among persons skilled or learned in agriculture. These neutral commissioners
were in addition to the 20 elected commissioners and could only be
seated provided each of them was unanimously approved by the elected
members. In this fashion 230 neutral commissioners were seated.

A great majority of both village and prefectural commissioners
were working farmers with the barest knowledge of administrative
procedures and government red tape. It was planned that they should
meet periodically because farm duties prevented commissioners from
remaining permanently on duty. Consequently, a secretariat of technicians and clerks was required to provide continuity of committee
functions. This secretariat, appointed by the commission, was in

effect its operating arm. Local commissions then usually had a full-time working staff of three people. Prefectural commissions employed as many as six. These administrative employees represented the authority of the commission and were informally vested with a wide latitude of responsibility.

The Central Agricultural Land Commission

The make-up of the central agricultural land commission acting as advisor on land reform matters to the Minister of Agriculture put the full stamp of democratic action on the entire Commission system. The 23 members of this body were appointed on March 27, 1947, on the recommendations of the Minister of Agriculture. Eight members of the central body were working tenants and eight more were landowners. Together these represented the eight administrative regions into which Japan is divided. Two members represented farm organizations and five others were learned and skilled in agriculture.

The people who made up this group symbolized as individuals the great change in the official composition and policy of the post surrender Japanese government. A woman, Chieko Sato of Shizuoka ken was one of the eight landowner representatives. Her appointment to a responsible position in government was one of the first of its kind to be accorded women in the modern history of Japan. Dr. Yasuo Kondo of Tokyo Imperial University, appointed as a person learned and skilled in agriculture, had already paid heavily in former years for this recognition with a prison term as the price of his liberal and democratic views on the needs of Japanese agriculture. But Dr. Kondo was not the only member of this group to have suffered repressive terrorism. Indeed, five of the eight tenant representatives had all served prison sentences for the sin of taking responsible leadership in movements to improve the conditions of the peasants.

This step, then, completed the machinery for carrying out the land reform program. Mention should perhaps be made of the occasional part-time employment of *buraku* assistants to the local commissions. These appointments were more or less honorary recognition for which the workers received little more than out-of-pocket expenses. Their services provided a valuable auxiliary resource.

The entire structure, going down from the capital, commenced with a central administrative group, advised by a central commission of farmers. This central body tied into 46 prefectural administrations through the Regional Land Offices. The prefectural governments, in turn, through *gun* organizations, served the rural population through 11,000 city, town, and village organizations. Coming up from the farmers were the 11,000 Village Land Commissions whose work was reviewed and endorsed by 46 Prefectural Land Commissions. Such was the organization planned to perform the land reform project. To a very considerable degree it succeeded in meeting the original purpose. In so doing, it achieved for the masses of the Japanese peasantry a remarkable degree of direct participation in the affairs of their government.

Chapter 10

DESIGN OF THE PROGRAM

S PRING is a peculiarly Japanese season. It seems a time especially
created for the people of that "flowery kingdom." True, all the
world rejoices with the harbingers of that auspicious period, but the
Japanese exult quietly in almost every detail of evidence of spring's
arrival. Each bud, each new bit of green, every vagrant breeze, and
the trillings of the different insect chorals are recognized and ac-
claimed with joy. The grandeur of the greening mountain sides and the
clouds which obscure Fujiyama have special names and meaning. New
leaves of the bamboo pass through a whole scale of coloring and so the
effect is called "the autumn of the bamboo." Wide areas of hillside
and valley take on the vivid color of the azalea, which grows wild in
Japan.

It is the beginning of the monsoon period, too, signifying the end of
the grim struggle with winter's bitter frost while extending the promise of new growth and another harvest.   Spring also brings the boon
of greater physical comfort. For the Japanese, beset with the choice
of designing homes to protect against the cold or to enhance the natural
beauties of spring and summer, have accepted no compromise. The
Japanese home is a summer house. It is a dwelling carefully planned
to aid in the appreciation of nature. Winter is the time of sacrifice
and discomfort, repaid by the pleasures of the milder seasons. So
spring, particularly, is the happy time for these island folk who mark
its infinite variations and accompaniments with colorful celebrations
and ceremonies.

All the charm of the period is most genuinely felt and most quaintly
expressed among rural folk. Each farm family becomes, with spring,
a conclave of poets and sentimentalists. Sliding partitions are opened
wide on vistas of tiny gardens. By the magic of Japanese landscaping
these pocket-sized arbors become a fairyland of fancy. One squats on
the rush matting in the room, but just inside the eaves, and silently
contemplates this microcosm of greenery through the muted light of a
gentle rain. A tiny hill of lawn is bordered by a thread of brook which
descends to a little pool. Here the red-gold carp dwell, and beside it
stands an old stone lantern. Children sit silently, intent on the song
of the cricket in the corner by a flowering plum. Old folk dream hap-
pily, thankful for release from the pains of winter, hopeful for the
reprieve which spring seems to promise.

Though fresh and green, the season is long overcast and wet. Fujiyama, so dominant in the crystalline winter days, is almost permanently shrouded in vapor and cloud masses. Fields turn green with the new wheat, but they are also extremely muddy. In places the whole countryside is so moist as to be swamplike, and the veils of rain trail endlessly inland across the long Pacific swells. So the charm and lightness of the season must come largely from the people themselves, who, in some mysterious way, have fashioned a quaint and lovely world out of rain, the commonplaces of the vernal equinox, and from the mundane realities of village life.

No one who has entered the well-nigh sacred precincts of a spring season in rural Japan would wish to change it to something else. It cannot be reduced to specific scientific terms and it cannot be reproduced artificially. It escapes analysis perhaps, because its appeal is in part mystical. The intermingled whole of people, of climate, and of the material environment seems to approach what the ecologists call a climax, that optimum adjustment between environment and the life, botanical and biological, which it sustains. Unfortunately, this development has also produced an inequitable set of property and social relations among the villagers. Yet, from another aspect, the culture has achieved many harmonies which stimulate and cherish ethics and esthetics of a high order. A plan to change the ordering of forces which had produced this Japanese tree of life required not only great justification but the assurance of a satisfactory outcome.

The Social and Political Challenge

These were the requirements which the architects and planners of the land reform program contemplated in that spring of 1947. Would the land reform project be sufficiently selective in its cultural and social effects within the village? Would it preserve and strengthen the forces which gave unique values to Japanese life while releasing the individual from thralldom? For now, the machine so painfully designed and constructed was primed for action. Once set in motion, its course was fateful. There could be no turning back. Nor was there time for major readjustment or correction if things went wrong. The plan as a whole had to function mainly according to original designs and anticipations or the resulting havoc would far outweigh any contemplated benefits. However, there was comfort in the thought that almost all the contingencies that human foresight could envision had been recognized in planning the operation of the program.

Indeed, it was the effort made to balance goals of the reform with preservation of principal outlines of the village culture which made the program unique — and difficult to plan.

The displacement of village leadership traditionally based on control of land could not be other than a distinct shock to an established system of life. Would the new leadership prove wise and moderate? More important still, would it appear and mature quickly enough to fill the vacuum left by the older leadership? Could the surgery of land transfer be accomplished without leaving permanent scars? Would the dispossessed landlord group foment strife, producing a cleavage to rip the social fabric? These and many other problems had been analyzed, and while many calculated risks were inherent in the final plan, yet specific allowance had been made for all the more important problems.

Already the American specialists had discouraged initial Japanese concepts of the reform as a punitive measure. The program as finally designed accented destruction of the institution of tenancy but explicitly discouraged any fomentation of class conflict. Again and again, Occupation personnel had pounded home the point that the program must bring about a release but not a revolution. The purpose was adjustment, not disruption. Pent-up forces of change and progress must be freed, but the essentially stable qualities of village life must be preserved. Ideals of justice and individual liberty must replace the mythical unreality of the "bright village." Conditions of growth and development both for the group and for individuals must be sought through a more equitable distribution of private property. Dislocation and the disordering of life must be avoided. The conduct of the reform through the agencies of government should, under no conditions, result in a strengthening of the power of the state over the individual.

Compared to these complex considerations, woven into the basic plan of the Japanese Land Reform Program, Communistic agrarian doctrines appear crude, simple, quick, and spurious. Such revolutionary reforms are almost instantaneous in their effectiveness. One day the landlords are in – the next day they are out. Former landowners are lucky to escape the turnover with their lives. All values of the old order are swept away in a roaring torrent of revolution and disorder. Individual rights and cultural heritage alike appear to be forgotten beside the irresistible novelty of collectivist doctrines. No time is lost in planning either legislation, administration, or program. Since, by Communist doctrine, the old order has no positive virtues, nothing of it need be saved and anything new is good – at least for the time being. Such programs result in chaos and continue in disorder over decades, until the state in despair expropriates irrevocably the whole national lands, or until a counterrevolution restores the old order with all its original injustices. Indeed from the cultivator's standpoint, the final outcome is merely trading one set of reactionary landlords for another.

The whole production and distribution process is disordered, with widespread starvation not an infrequent accompaniment. As production problems become more and more acute, quick and easy solutions, mostly of a violent nature, are sought. Peasants whose only crime is bewilderment are shot, banished, or imprisoned in vast numbers. Compared to the promptness of Communist land reforms, the type of reform undertaken in Japan appears to suffer by contrast because of the slow rate of its initial progress. Beside the vast upheavals of revolutionary land redistribution schemes, a carefully planned redistribution program is quiet in the initial stages and apparently not very newsworthy.

For these reasons it was perhaps to be expected that the Soviet press and Communist journalism generally would seize on the delays of the legislative and planning phases of the Japanese program. The delays were presented as the result of capitalist inefficiency. The selective aspects of the program were contrasted with the universal reforms in Poland and Eastern Germany which, it was boasted, were carried out in a few weeks. Although there had not been a definite breach in relations and while the Soviet Union was still an official member of the Allied Occupation, Moscow did not hesitate to avow openly its disbelief in the sincerity of the Occupation program.

There was a very good reason for these actions. For behind it all was the underlying challenge of the Japanese reform to Soviet ambitions in Asia. Everywhere in Asia, land and rights to land are at the heart of all social, economic, and political questions. The people of Asia are, in the overwhelming majority, farmers. So all politics finally comes down to the question of land and its control. If Communist prestige was to remain high in Asia, it would do so primarily because of its land policy. In this context a reform of Japanese land institutions based on private property, emphasizing individual rights and responsibilities, while denying the upheaval and distress of revolution, might appeal to the Asiatic masses. Such an appeal would be a threat to the long-drawn plans of Moscow.

Moreover, almost the entire history of Japanese Communist activity, most of its aims and ambitions, centered on agrarian reforms. In fact, land reform had for long been the special political property of the Japanese Communists. If the reform were successfully accomplished, it would pull the rug out from under the entire Communist position in Japan. Finally, such a reform conducted in non-Marxist terms and stressing individual rights, private property, and auxiliary capitalist concepts could embarrass the Communist position throughout the world.

The Economic Challenge

In these circumstances of world political competition, both the Japanese and the Occupation were playing for high stakes. On the one hand, the reform program must be thoroughly effective in canceling out the ancient landlord system; on the other, it must demonstrate that democratic social and political action could be vigorous without becoming disruptive or destructive. Moreover, the program had to be completely genuine in and for itself. It could not be a synthetic demonstration or a political coup. Adding it all up, this amounted to no easy task.

Take, for example, Yoshida village in Shimane prefecture. Arthur Raper, of the United States Department of Agriculture, has pointed out

that a single land-owning family had dominated the life of Yoshida for
over 700 years.[1] Farm houses, cultivated land, forest land, even livestock and sometimes farm tools were rented by the tenants from this
family. An atmosphere of deference and subservience toward this
dominant group pervaded all the affairs of the village. Thus, all
leadership, all protection, and all security in Yoshida emanated from
a single hereditary group. This family paid a large share (over 70%)
of all taxes and was the major contributor to several village temples
and shrines. So extensive was its wealth that a tenant never dealt
directly with the family but always through a hierarchy of retainers
and sublandlords. Could Yoshida, as a community, absorb the impact
of land reform which would sweep away almost this entire source of
leadership? Would the new independent owners face up to sharing
their full part of the obligations formerly borne by the central family?
This was the test which the land reform program must face, not only
in Yoshida but throughout rural Japan.

Aside from these somewhat long-range considerations there was
the immediate practical question of the program's effect on agricultural production. In 1947 the Japanese food situation was still critical.
National starvation had been narrowly averted and a long period of inadequate diet lay yet ahead for all the people. Trains running to and
from the great metropolitan centers were still crammed with city
folk. These people poured into the countryside hoping to buy food
directly from the farmers. Although this traffic was illegal – an
aspect of the black market – major business establishments and even
government offices permitted their employees time off for these ex-
peditions.

Despite moral and legal sanctions, this simple visceral reaction
to hunger was almost universal. For the time being, attempts at
police control were largely ineffective. Occasionally, a whole train
was stopped at the outskirts of some large city and raided by the
police. The agony of the passengers as their precious bundles were
unrolled and confiscated on the station platform was unforgettably
sad. Their sheer hopelessness as they crowded into trucks for a ride
to the nearest police station affected everyone who saw it including
the police. Of course, with the black market went inflation and with
inflation further economic instability. For this reason all efforts to
stabilize the Japanese economy and start the nation on the road to
recovery were turned to a great degree to increasing the amount and
efficiency of agricultural production.

Production quotas for rice and other staple crops were drawn up
by the government and assigned to each village. The sum of these
quotas at planting time in 1947 with some possible emergency supple-
mentation from American imports represented the entire anticipated
national food supply until the harvest of 1948. Nothing, not even the

---

[1]Arthur F. Raper *et al.*, *The Japanese Village in Transition,* Report No. 136 (Tokyo:
Natural Resources Section, G.H.Q., S.C.A.P.), p. 140.

desirable objectives of land reform, could be permitted to interfere
with the accomplishment of this production goal, for on that depended
existence itself. Consequently, this factor too had to be carefully
integrated in the plans of the reform operations.

The history of land reform in other countries after World War I
was not an inspiring memory. In the Soviet Union, in the Balkans,
and in Hungary these reforms, almost without exception, had been
accompanied by a drastic fall in the production of essential foodstuffs.
Harvest deficiencies, the resulting starvation, and the dislocation of
the European countries had prolonged the miserable aftermath of war,
delayed postwar reconstruction and increased political instability.
This could not be permitted to occur in Japan.

Then the resident landlords had to be considered. These families
could not be cast adrift to sink or swim. The principal economic
problem of this segment arose among those landlords whose loss of
income from sale of their land might be disastrous. Fortunately there
were many of these who had continued to farm a small tract as owner-
operators. Still others had claims for support on grown sons and
daughters. A number were small businessmen in the village. For the
remainder there was the new Social Security and Old Age Assistance
Law and the possibility that the compensation paid for their land under
the reform program could be invested in nonagricultural ventures.
Yet it could hardly be expected in these cases that an equivalent return could be realized.

Nonresident landlords were a different matter. To many of these,
landed property was an impersonal investment, along with other business property, paying perhaps a larger dividend than most other investments, but still just another investment. Many people in this
group had already made the transition out of village life. They had
long since become adjusted to metropolitan living. Their energies
and loyalties had, even before the war, been transferred to other
fields. No particular shock to village life would result from breaking
their last tie with the village.

In either case, however, land owned by landlords could not be
seized arbitrarily. It had to be purchased in an orderly fashion. The
law provided a process for determining the price of each parcel. This
price, based on an official formula, was to be paid by the government
to the legal owner. According to this formula a "rental value" based
on actual rental history was set in 1938 for each piece of agricultural
land in Japan. This value was supposed to be set every ten years but
as a war and postwar emergency measure the value was frozen like
all other prices. To obtain the price of a particular piece of land, its
rental value was multiplied by an official factor which was supposed
to represent time. Thus the legal price of paddy land was, according
to this formula, the annual rental value for 40 years; the price of upland fields was 48 years at the annual rental value. The average
national price for paddy fields, according to this formula, was approxi-
mately 3,400 yen per acre; for upland, 1,800 yen per acre. Local

land commissions had the task of working out these computations and within perscribed limits could make adjustments to meet individual situations.

These factors had to be fitted into the plan of the reform. For some problems a reasonably satisfactory outcome could be anticipated. In other instances, as for example, questions of leadership and village solidarity, a degree of risk was inevitable. The fate of the landlord group had to be tempered by mercy and common-sense judgment. In the case of production no risks were permissible. Thus throughout the entire program a degree of flexibility was indispensable so that agriculture and rural life were not unrealistically constricted in a rigid framework. The basic meaning of the reform was conceived to lie, not in impersonal categories of theoretical reform, but in the essential needs of human flesh and blood.

Legal Framework of the Reform

No matter how just a law may be, it has always to be interpreted. Public administrators are fallible like other men. So the principle of adequate appeal procedures from both legal interpretation and the decisions of officials was indispensable in the land reform program. This salutary principle was designed to insure justice under the law for individuals who objected to any act in connection with the purchase or sale of land. The very existence of an appeal procedure was expected to act as a brake on official action and a deterrent to haste and carelessness. While persons with a grievance against the acts of the local commission were granted sufficient time to make their appeals, the appeals had to be made promptly. They could not be used as a device for confusing or obstructing the work of the commission over an extended period. Likewise, decisions on appeals had to be made promptly. No action to buy or sell land under the program was permissible if any appeal relative to the transaction was unsettled.

Within the framework of the law each village was expected to recognize and solve its own problems. Administratively each village was treated as a separate entity. Problems of one village were not permitted to become the burden of another. There was to be no mass movement or resettlement of people across village lines. This meant that the over-all pattern of land use and the distribution of arable land might not be disturbed.

Villages in which there were a large number of cultivators and a small area of farm land would continue to have small farms. Larger farm units in the northern Honshu prefectures of Aomori and Iwate, where individual units averaged seven to nine acres, would not change their typical size. Farmers of Nisi Susa village in Shimae ken would continue to cultivate 1.7 acres on the average and those in Nadabun village down on the plain would, on a somewhat ampler scale, farm about 2.5 acres each. The land reform program could not change the amount of arable land nor the village population. Moreover, the relation between cultivated land and the compost rights on neighboring grass and forest lands had been adjusted through centuries to arable land requirements. The combination of population, cultivated land, forest rights, grassland rights, water rights, and drainage require-ments was the intricate product of a very long experience. A disturb-ance of these relations had no place in the reform program. Rather it was a function of that project to preserve the combination.

In large degree, tenants would become owners of the same land which they had rented. Even in the case of the few very large land-owners, like the Homma family of Sakata in Yamagata ken, the land-lord customarily parceled out his land in very small tracts to the tenants. Hence the principal effect of the reform plan on the Homma holdings would be with respect to ownership. Probably no one would move physically to or from the Homma land. A considerable number of farmers would continue to cultivate the same land, perhaps a little more, perhaps a little less. There would be exceptions. Some trans-fers would have to be made between tenants with the results that in the final reshuffle some tenants would acquire a part of their original land along with some additional tracts to supplement land which in turn would be transferred to a neighboring tenant. However, all these transfers were to take place within the village.

There was to be no "land rush" reminiscent of the Indian Territory and Cherokee Strip in the United States. Each applicant who wished to purchase land in the village would first of all have to be a genuine resident of the village and an established farmer. Second, he would have to be able to prove to the local commission's satisfaction that he was a tenant. Then his capacity as a cultivator would be carefully considered. Regardless of the outcome, it was unlikely that a tenant would be able to purchase much more land than he had ordinarily rented. This was due to the fact that the enlargement of one small holding could only result in the diminution of another. Moreover, no person, whether tenant or owner-operator, would be permitted under the law to acquire or to retain a holding larger than the average legal maximum established for the area. Maximum holdings in the south and west would be very small with somewhat larger maximums pre-vailing in the north and east.

Each resident landlord was permitted to retain a small amount of land which he could continue to rent. The legal maximum of such land was set at 2.5 acres. Again this national maximum was subject to regional variations, and in any event, the aggregate amount of all such land in Japan could not exceed ten per cent of the total arable land. Rental arrangements on this land were subject to very strict require-ments. These requirements were enforced by the local commission which also supervised the transaction in considerable detail.

The purpose of this residual rental area was twofold: It provided partial relief to resident landlords, but also it benefited owner-cultivators who might temporarily need to rent out land which they owned. On the other hand, it might aid a farmer who for a short time had a legitimate need for a small additional increment to his established holding. It was intended by this device of controlled rentals to preserve a degree of flexibility for the solution of farm management problems which would be lost if all land were placed in the strait jacket of universal ownership. For example, an owner-cultivator might fall ill and for a short time be unable to cultivate his land. If all leasing were prohibited, the land in such instances would go out of production.

Under the reform program, however, all leasing of land was subject to strict public regulation. Landlords and tenants were not free to make independent contracts. Nor was either party free to terminate a lease without the express permission of the local commission. Each such lease was reduced to writing. For this purpose the Ministry of Agriculture worked out a model lease for use throughout Japan, fashioned after a standard lease form prepared by the U. S. Department of Agriculture. The amount of the rent, term of lease, sharing of expenses, responsibility for improvements, etc., were all specified in the lease. The conditions and negotiations leading up to execution of the lease were all carefully supervised by the local commission. This new procedure was based on the modern legal theory of contracts in contrast to the former feudal right doctrine.

It was anticipated that the experience gained by the tenant members of the land commissions would stimulate the development of leadership from this important but hitherto unvocal group. Of course, no one knew precisely what to expect from them. In certain villages there would doubtless be some uninhibited "smart alecks" who would take advantage of the new situation to indulge their egos and cause embarrassment to their constituents. It was hoped that such types would be promptly recalled. However, the greater part of the tenant commissioners would be bashful and confused. For this reason the program was designed to give the commissioners as much experience as possible in the initial stages without overburdening them. If these men responded satisfactorily, a great deal of the uncertainty concerning leadership would be resolved.

Time Schedule of the Reform

A significant feature of the land transfer operation was its carefully planned timing. Duties of the village land commissions were very heavy. Yet, as individuals, the members of these bodies were for the most part working farmers. It was necessary to schedule their work on the commissions in such a way that it did not interfere with farming operations. Their duties were largely concerned with the selection of land under the law and its transfer from one ownership to another.

Tanaka-san could not be expected to sit all day in commission meetings at planting time nor at any of the other critical dates on his agricultural calendar. Tanaka-san in these busy periods worked very hard from dawn to dark. He could not, therefore, be expected to stay late at the village office engaged in official duties. For these reasons the government designed an operating program fitted to the seasonal needs of farmers. This program established a schedule of dates on which land was to be transferred. These dates were: March 31, 1947; July 2, 1947; October 2, 1947; December 31, 1947; March 2, 1948; July 2, 1948; October 2, 1948; December 31, 1948.

Everyone hoped to be able to finish transfers of land by December 31, 1948. Japanese bureaucrats estimated that the transfer would total about four million acres. Occupation people from their own observations concluded that a somewhat larger amount would finally be transferred. The latter prediction proved accurate. Estimated amounts of land available for transfer to tenants was allocated among the several scheduled dates with larger quotas established in the slack agricultural periods. In earlier periods and during busier seasons smaller and lighter tasks were set.

Earlier purchase dates, March 31 and July 2, 1947, were expected to provide a "breaking-in" period for inexperienced commissioners. Both amounts and types of land selected for acquisition on these dates were designed to educate without discouraging these novices in public affairs. For the first transfer date, March 31, 1947, a national quota of 316,684 acres was established and an additional 405,455 acres was set as a goal for the second transfer on the following July 2. Lands to be acquired on these dates were designated in classes of ownership likely to cause the fewest problems and perplexities. These were, for the most part, lands owned by nonresident landlords. All such lands were clearly subject to Land Reform Law without reservation. They presented no complexities nor borderline cases — the bane of official decisions. The commission's task was then a simple straightforward job of verifying ownership records and physically locating the lands. Tenant lands owned by temples and shrines fell in a similar legal class and were also included in the early purchase plans.

In the three-month interval between transfer dates each commission prepared its "plan." This plan included all land which a commission recommended for transfer on a specific date. Hence these plans were basic documents in land transfer operations. At the commencement of each period the commission, having a clearly established quota to meet, selected a number of tracts of land based on the apparent legal status of each separate parcel. These parcels were spotted on a map which became an important part of the plan. Next a careful check of records was made. Ownership, location, boundaries, and actual terms of tenant cultivation were then determined by the commission clerks with aid from semiofficial *buraku* assistants. When all details of this nature had been assembled, the whole commission formally considered the matter and reached a decision.

Such meetings were public. The commission heard witnesses and took testimony from all concerned. It finally published the plan by posting it on the village bulletin board. Within 10 days all appeals from the plan had to be filed. The commission must settle an appeal within 20 days of the expiration of the initial 10-day appeal period. Petitioners, if still dissatisfied, could appeal over the head of the local commission to the prefectural land commission within 10 days of the local decision, and prefectural commissions then had 20 days to settle cases. In all, a petitioner had 60 days in which to appeal his case and obtain a decision. In this period no final action could be taken with regard to his rights. If appeals were still pending on a particular parcel at the time of an approaching purchase period, there was no alternative but to omit it from the plan. It could be inserted in a subsequent plan after a decision on the appeal had been reached, or dropped as the case might be. Decisions of the commission were in the form of recommendations to Prefectural Land Commissions. Thus final plans were summaries of recommendations reached by commissions in a particular transfer period.

Several days prior to the end of a transfer period the village plan was complete. Messengers from each village, by train, bicycle, or bus, carried completed plans to the prefectural capital and officially presented them to the Prefectural Land Commission. In the time remaining, prefectural secretariats carefully checked the plans presented by each village against the law, for arithmetical errors and inconsistencies. On the final day, the transfer date, prefectural commissions announced their decision for each village plan. All lands whose transfer was officially approved were automatically certified by the Prefectural Governor as agent for the national government and this formally accomplished the transfer. Title to the land then vested in the government. Local commission recommendations found to be incorrect or which the prefectural commission failed to approve were returned to the village for correction and further study. Village representatives who had attended the prefectural commission sessions returned home and announced the final results. The decision was then posted on official village bulletin boards at village offices.

Establishment of a series of dates and land transfer quotas was the chief means of insuring accomplishment of the over-all task. These schedules and quotas seemed to be about the only tools suitable for controlling a very large number of workers who were, at best, rather loosely organized. Whatever else a village commission might desire to do, it was always confronted with the need for accomplishing a certain fixed amount of work in a specified time. Moreover, work had to be arranged so that adequate time for appeals was available. Again, in the interest of allowing the newly formed commissions a shake-down period they were not required in the earlier stages to buy and sell land simultaneously. At first all activity was concentrated on the purchase of land. Thus the earlier plans were exclusively *purchase plans*. The purchaser was the government and the procedure for this step was relatively simple. Subsequent resale to tenants of the land which the government thus acquired was designed as a later phase of the program.

Like a staircase with gradually increased risers between steps the plan of land reform operations was designed to fit needs of village commissioners. Smaller burdens and simpler problems in initial periods allowed these officials to gain familiarity and confidence for heavier burdens and more complex problems of later periods. Thus it was particularly fortunate that the law provided a two-stage land transfer operation with land purchased first by government and later resold by government to designated tenant. While this meant doubling the number of transactions it also enabled inexperienced commissioners to concentrate on one task at a time. This method also avoided a direct conflict between individual tenants and their landlords. In the initial step, title to the landlord's land passed to the government. Consequently, a landlord could protest against the purchase of his land without involving a particular tenant. Thus personal differences and animosities between landlords and tenants were avoided; moreover, the commission could proceed in its deliberations without need for arbitrating personal feuds.

Once the decision to purchase land from a particular landlord was reached after full debate and title had passed to the state, the landlord had no further interest in the subsequent disposal of his land. For this reason purchases were always made considerably in advance of sales. Initially this meant that government acquired a considerable land inventory before any sales were made to the tenants. Tenants eager to become owners simply had to bide their anxiety. In the interim between purchase and sale the land was operated by the tenant whose landlord was now the government.

At this time and distance these various devices seem so simple and self-evident that their mention appears almost superfluous. Yet each of them was the product of careful planning and analysis. Together they amounted to a very dextrous scheme for avoiding class conflict, preserving village solidarity, maintaining valuable cultural aspects, avoiding interference with agricultural production, training local commissioners, and assuring an orderly progress of operations. All of these measures required time to work out. Communist publicists, if they chose, could attribute these delays to bad faith and inefficiency. Occupation specialists viewed the thorough consideration of these matters as an indispensable prerequisite to the success of a reform conducted in terms of securing a wider distribution of the ownership of land and the up-grading of individual rights in the rural areas of Japan.

Chapter 11

PROBLEMS AND PROGRESS

ESSENTIALLY the success or failure of the reform of the Japanese land tenure system depended on the disposition of tenant loyalties. If tenants wished to become freemen and property owners, they must break the ties that held them in thralldom to the landlords. While the loss of the war had greatly shaken the older loyalties, yet the displacement was only preliminary and partial. New loyalties must be developed to the new leadership which must arise if the reform was to be effective. Particularly must tenants be willing to support their representatives on the Village Land Commissions. For these reasons the central strategy of the opposing interests involved in the reform was built around a struggle for tenant loyalties. Psychologically the landlord group had a considerable initial advantage. On the other hand, the appeal of land ownership was a deep-seated and powerful urge.

Landlord Opposition

This central issue of tenant loyalties found concrete symbolism in the Village Land Commission. Thus this body soon became a principal object of landlord attack. The commissions were the forcing beds for the new agrarian leadership around which the new village loyalties must cluster. However, cause and effect were intermingled in this respect. In order to evoke loyalty the tenant commissioners must demonstrate leadership. Yet the village system had traditionally discouraged development of leadership traits among the smaller farmers. Aside from a few regions, tenant organization and tenant leadership in the postwar years was almost nonexistent. Hence it was necessary simply to hope that both leadership traits and decisions as to loyalties would develop favorably as the program unfolded. Progress in the accomplishment of the reform would be an index of the extent of the validity of these assumptions. A slowly moving program would probably connote a confused and frightened tenancy slipping back into feudal patterns or successfully intimidated by traditional leaders.

In this contest landlord interests would continue earlier efforts seeking to justify the status quo. They would increase their emphasis on the merits of feudalism and of the ancient traditions. A victory for these concepts would have a profound influence not only in rural Japan but on the ultimate meaning of the Occupation for all Japan. Indeed agrarian reform highlighted issues of a struggle which in a larger context began at Pearl Harbor. A victory for landlords connoted the reaffirmation of a static, inequitable relation in rural villages. But additionally, considering the significance of the issue, opposition to reform was also a maneuver by which to express dissent from the basic concepts of the Occupation. So land reform was a rallying point for all Japanese who recognized its wider significance for a new democratic Japan.

The results of the first land purchase concluded on March 31, 1947, were not reassuring to the proponents of the reform. On that date a goal of 316,684 acres had been planned for purchase. This goal was a minimum and should have been exceeded. But only slightly more than 300,000 acres were actually acquired. In addition, the spottiness of returns was even more alarming. Several important prefectures reported only token gestures of compliance. For example, Kanagawa prefecture adjacent to Tokyo, Miyazaki on Kyushu, and Kagawa on Shikoku had purchased only 1,027 acres from a combined area eligible for purchase of nearly 125,000 acres. Hundreds and hundreds of village commissions in these prefectures had made no purchases at all. So in these villages, opposition among recalcitrant landlords had successfully prevented action by the land commissions. Since tenants had half the votes on the commissions, there was a strong presumption that tenant members of the commissions had either voted with the landlords against purchase, had failed to vote, or had not attended the commission meetings.

Yet one could hardly blame the commissioners. Tenant constituents were uncertain and half-hearted in their support. Many tenants were thinking: "I would be most happy to become a landowner if ownership is possible for me. But until I am much more sure than I am now that this is possible, I must maintain intact my relationship with the land-owning families from whom I rent land." In the spring of 1947, tenants in southern Japan villages were reported as saying they were not sure they wanted to own land. When questioned by Occupation investigators, several tenants said they "feared they might not be able to become landowners." Thus tenant commissioners had little assurance of support in a real test of strength with the landlords. Moreover, tenant commissioners and their families faced grave personal problems if landlord reprisals were directed against them. The least of these would surely entail severe economic sanctions.

Then, too, emotional odds were heavily weighted against them. As they sat in the village hall, they had only to glance up at the portraits of former village officials to become acutely aware that as tenant farmers they were profaning precincts never entered by commoners in all village history. Extremely ill at ease, they confronted across the conference table haughty scions of venerable families, their traditional superiors, whose forebears had for centuries symbolized pride, dignity, and prestige.

A village land commission meeting, Yokogoshi, Niigata prefecture. (Courtesy, U. S. Army.)

And now that the chips were down, numbers of landlords fully exploited this prestige. In 1945 and 1946 there had been a scattering of
landlord aggressions, but these were merely anticipative. The situation now became decisive. It was win or lose. In Fukuoka prefecture
in southern Japan, landlords inspired whole villages to accept anew
time-honored beliefs that landlord-tenant relations should be discussed
only within the *buraku*. These affairs, so they claimed, were intimate
and personal, not to be indecently exposed to public debate. Of course,
in such *buraku* meetings "the voices of the tenants would have been
neglected; if the tenants oppose it, they would be in general threatened
with ostracism as the peace disturber."

In Yunomae town of Kumamoto prefecture the Village Land Commission was unable to agree on a chairman, so the prefectural governor appointed a tenant, Takeoku Oka. Oka had an unusual reputation
as a tenant leader and a land reform enthusiast. Apparently he was a
diligent man because, in the preparation of the July 2, 1947, purchase
plan, he found that important records unfavorable to certain landlords
were missing or stolen. He instituted an investigation. He advised
some tenants to cease paying rent to their landlords in kind (i.e., in
rice which was illegal rather than in cash at legal rates). Accordingly,
several tenants deposited the legal amount of cash in the village de-
pository.

Immediately a smear campaign commenced. Oka was called a
Communist, although he was not. Several landlord groups then pro-
tested his appointment to the prefectural governor. The governor,
frightened by the uproar, stated that he had nothing to do with the appointment – did not even know who the chairman was. Landlords then
charged in the local court that, since Oka's appointment was illegal,
his acts as chairman of the commission were also illegal. The court
issued an injunction suspending the chairman. Immediately rebellious
landlords posted public notices that the land purchase plan worked up
under Oka's chairmanship was invalid. The matter was finally
straightened out and Oka was reinstated. But the incident brought the
land reform program in Yunomae town to a complete halt for over a
month and badly demoralized the tenants.

In Oita prefecture at Minami-Innai-mura, landlord Yoshida administered a beating to his tenant, Edo. This landlord had "taken back"
land leased to his tenant while the tenant was absent in the army.
However, the female members of the tenant's family had continued to
farm the land. The commission had intervened in the dispute, ruling
that half the original land should be returned to the tenant, but the
prefectural governor ruled that all the land originally rented should
be returned to him. However, the landlord refused to return the land
to Edo and, after repeated petitions by Edo, became violent and beat
him. The significant point in this affair was the failure of any official
body to *enforce* the return of the land to the tenant. The police took
no action in Edo's behalf even after the beating and the land commission simply threw up its hands in despair after Yoshida's failure to
comply with its weak-kneed finding.

These were not isolated cases; there were many more like them. The local police attended land commission meetings at Miyata village in Kumamoto. They admonished tenant commissioners to hold their peace. A number of landlords at Tayoda village also in Kumamoto sought to induce the village assembly to reduce the salary of the Village Land Commission clerk in an effort to force his resignation. Landlords of Miyazaki prefecture assaulted tenants in Shiwadi-mura and in another village denied tenants access to compost fields. In Kagoshima prefecture one Ogata, a judge, delivered a resounding opinion against land reform. He then resigned to become an attorney for a group of landlords.

Kagoshima prefecture is the ancient seat of the famous Shimazu clan which had ruled a large portion of this Kyushu prefecture since the thirteenth century. Prior to the Restoration of 1868 the clan was one of the acknowledged rulers of Japan; but an official of the Ministry of Agriculture and Forestry who visited the family seat saw little difference between the attitude of the modern and of the feudal Shimazu clan. In somewhat awkward English he observed: "But even after the Restoration there has been no change to be seen in their traditional way of thinking as far as today, even if the squire (feudal lord) system had already changed to the relations of the land-owner and the tenant as it was after the Restoration (1868). Thus the tenants, the common people of farmers descent, would obey anything whatever the landlord, the military class of samurai or warrior descent would say, treading faithfully in their ancestors' footsteps without little knowing how to break through the hard crust of conventionalism. Such being the circumstance, the tenants, even now where the farm land reform is carried out, are rather spiritless than powerless, they are inclined to avoid disputes with the landlords even though they would be treated unjustly."

These illustrations have all been drawn from the island of Kyushu, yet military government observers at Akita in northeastern Honshu observed that "the tenants do not seem to consider the landlords capable of doing wrong." Newspapers somewhat inaccurately reported acts of violence by landlords against tenants in Niigata prefecture and other aggressive acts in contravention of the law in Nagano in north central Honshu. So landlord harrassment was not confined to any special region. Rather it was sporadic all over Japan. Of course, these clashes were occasionally relieved by outstanding examples of landlord cooperation. But the majority of incidents were adverse.

Two salient features characterized these incidents: unwillingness or inability of many tenants to protect themselves against landlord aggression, and tacit approval of landlord excesses by the ruling village hierarchy including police and judiciary. This thumbing the nose at General MacArthur's agrarian policy apparently seemed, to numerous landlords and their henchmen, to be a fairly safe pastime.

Now it would have been simple to commit the power of the Occupation and thus to enforce compliance with the law. But this was a pitfall

to be carefully avoided because one such action might have placed all
further administration of the law squarely in the lap of the Occupation.
Meanwhile the duty of quiet observation was a grueling test of the
merits of patience to the responsible Occupation personnel. Yet the
price had to be paid. For American and Japanese planners alike
placed their faith in the effectiveness of the democratic process. And
those who make such pledges must have the courage of their convic-
tions. They have to learn that social processes do not work in a day
or in weeks, but that these forces do have a devastating momentum
when once the initial inertia is overcome.

Moreover, it was impossible to determine in these earlier months
whether the incidents of resistance were isolated events or whether
collectively, they indicated a trend. They might portend the beginning of a widespread integrated revolt. They might be merely the
rash acts of desperation. Yet apparently the Soviet Union thought it
knew how to interpret the landlord resistance. It launched an attack
on land reform policy, delegating as its prosecutor Lt. General
Kuzma Derevyanko, the Chief of the Soviet Mission to Japan.

Russian Obstructionist Tactics

General Derevyanko was an impressive man, constructed on heroic
lines. He radiated power. In the Soviet Union he probably enjoyed a
tremendous military reputation. His official position automatically
entitled him to membership on the Allied Council for Japan, where he
was a most colorful figure. In order to launch the Soviets' attack on
land reform, he introduced a number of official questions on the
progress of the reform as the agenda for the regular June 25, 1947,
meeting of the Allied Council. These questions were worded in the
not-unfamiliar "When did you stop beating your wife?" vein so characteristic of Soviet argumentation. Along these lines the General
wanted to know "How much land has been transferred to tenants?" and
"What is holding up the program?"

Now General Derevyanko was familiar with the principles, methods,
and machinery for carrying out the program. He had joined with the
Council in recommendations for its formulation and establishment.
He knew all about the date, December 31, 1948, established for official
completion of the program. He had been a party to setting the date.
Consequently, his faultfinding after a bare six months had elapsed
could only be interpreted as a purely political move to embarrass the
United States. The General's questions suggested that land reform
was a sorry mess. He hinted at sabotage, not by the Japanese but by
the Occupation. It appeared to the General that the program was
moving at a pace inconsistent with honest intent. All the General's
questions were answered fully and completely.

But apparently the answers pleased neither the General nor the
Kremlin. They showed that a great deal of progress had been made in
developing the groundwork of a thoroughgoing agrarian reconstruction

of Japan. The implied charges of sabotage and lack of integrity were specifically demolished. So, considering everything, General Derevyanko's criticism of land reform succeeded in proving only substantial accomplishments and creditable speed. Frustrated in a first attempt, the Soviet Union apparently decided to try again. Once more General Derevyanko placed land reform on the agenda of the Allied Council for its July 23, 1947, meeting.

In the meantime, the July 2 land transfer had been made on schedule. Results were much more favorable than on the previous March. A goal of 405,455 acres had been scheduled, but final results showed that 553,301 acres had actually been acquired – more than 145,000 acres over the estimate! Together with the purchase of the previous March, the government had thus far acquired from landlords a cumulative total of 853,301 acres, later to be sold to tenants. Also purchases were much more uniformly distributed among the villages. Prefectures which had had poor records in March showed great improvement. Certainly things were going better in spite of General Derevyanko's contentions.

The July 23 meeting was an acrimonious affair. The American Ambassador, Mr. George Atcheson, at the outset made it clear that GHQ had no intention of being pushed around by the Soviet Union or its representatives. Neither GHQ nor the United States would tolerate any suggestion of the Soviets' right to challenge its policies or conduct.

Representatives of the United States and the British Commonwealth were plainly dressed civilians. The Chinese representative, a placid General, wore only the simplest military dress. But General Derevyanko was overwhelming in the full dress uniform of a high-ranking Soviet officer. His beautifully tailored white uniform with scarlet and gold trimmings glittered with decorations. The General bore himself with a most impressive military air.

Bustling around the Soviet representative was a numerous group of lesser officers, civilian interpreters, men of the Soviet press, and minor functionaries. In contrast to this display, Atcheson, with two assistants, seemed almost as lonely as did MacMahon Ball, the British representative, and the placid Chinese General. The bearing of the Soviet representative and the size of its delegation seemed clearly designed to create an atmosphere of power and domination.

It was quite an experience for the agricultural specialist assisting Mr. Atcheson to confront the awe-inspiring Soviet General. Yet the challenge proved not to be difficult. Fortunately an almost complete lack of facts or of any real knowledge of Japanese agriculture handicapped the General. His resounding charges fell pretty flat. Most of his statements of fact were disproved. Yet in the face of specific evidence to the contrary, General Derevyanko labored mightily. He dwelt at length on what he called half-way measures and a half-hearted program of reform. He made much of the fact that there was opposition among the landlords. He seemed to feel that this opposition was altogether audacious, unreasonable, and intolerable. He hinted that existence of opposition was evidence of a breakdown in administration of the program. He cited as fact several gross errors from the Japanese press. He misquoted the Land Reform Law and misinterpreted its meaning. He played up an isolated beating of a tenant by a landlord to create the impression that mass assaults were commonplace and that chaos existed throughout rural Japan. He overlooked completely the results of the July 2, 1947, land transfer and its implications of progress. This attack was followed by an attempt to allude to the advantages of a Soviet type land reform. At this point, however, Ambassador Atcheson suggested reading into the records several adverse accounts of Soviet agrarian experience from 1917 on. Here, the record indicates, Dr. Ball intervened as a peacemaker and the session ended.

Why did the Soviet Union make this attack? Why attack at this particular time? It seems likely, in the first place, that for reasons already stated, the Soviet Union could not have been happy as a partner to the Japanese land reform policy. The program was dedicated to the redistribution of land to the tenants but only as private property and within the framework of law. On the one hand, in Japan, the Soviet Union was tied to a non-Communist reform of agriculture, while in the Balkans, Poland, and Eastern Germany she was sponsoring orthodox Communist agrarian revolutions. Thus the attack on the Japanese program was an inevitable "straightening of the line." Then, since it was necessary for the Kremlin to repudiate the Japanese program, it was better to do it when an attack would be most harmful. So a time was selected when the program was thought to be involved in mounting difficulties. If this additional attack caused the program to fail, the tenants would have received a clear warning that only a reform on Communist lines could succeed.

Fortunately the whole affair miscarried. In fact it backfired badly because it served notice on the Japanese farmers of the Occupation's intent to support the program at all costs, even of offending the powerful Soviet Union. So one immediate result was to stimulate tenant morale. Another consequence arose from the clear implication that if "Reds" didn't like the program, then the reform could not be a "Red" operation. Its supporters could not be Communists. A further by-product of the Derevyanko incident was the opportunity it provided to sell the program anew, and this time with some tangible evidence of progress. So all in all, the Soviet attack on land reform, an appeal to tenant loyalties from the left, failed miserably.

Judicial Hindrances

In spite of these more favorable events, the law enforcement branch of government remained aloof from the program. Sometimes its personnel sided openly with the landlords. Frequently when cases involving landlords and tenants were presented, the courts turned to older statutes and precedents, pointedly ignoring the Land Reform Law.

Now Japanese judges and law enforcement officials belonged to a caste which was almost sacrosanct. This exalted state permitted them to remain far from the vulgar haunts of vulgar men. They simply disdained to notice the reform, as much because they despised innovations of any kind as because of bias toward tenants. One of the young Japanese agricultural officials pointed out: "Judges, in general, whose social as well as economical viewpoints basing upon the landlords' class are socially on intimate terms with the influential class. In this respect they are relied upon by such classes so that some of them hitherto have inclined to give sympathetic decisions upon the landlord class, being unable to cast off their old skins which have regarded what the tenants said as the dangerous thoughts and oppressed them accordingly." Military government officers on Kyushu reported along the same lines: "Landlords, however, prefer to take such matters before the local courts where, in most instances, they are assured of a more favorable interpretation of the law, the courts in many instances being extremely conservative."

Of course the principal point in land reform litigation was not the immediate transfer of ownership from landlord to tenant. That phase lay several months in the future. Rather, landlords wished simply to get rid of their tenants. As we have seen, they desired to get their land out of a rental category so it could not be classified as tenant-operated land. Thus the landlords and those allied with them sought other means, aside from the Land Reform Law, to regain possession of their land.

In a good many instances, in the first half year or so of the program, the courts, directly and indirectly, aided these attempts at evasion. In such cases they completely bypassed both the Land Reform Law and the commissions. A serious threat underlay these legalized evasions. Landlord leaders were endeavoring to crystallize landlord unrest into a cohesive national movement. They planned to use the precedent-making value of numerous judicial decisions adverse to the tenants and to the new law. If a large enough backlog of these decisions could be recorded, they anticipated a mass filing of cases covering entire regions or even the whole country − a sort of legalized revolt.

Another example of judicial indifference was the frequent granting of temporary restraining orders prohibiting entry of the tenants to disputed lands. This was a diabolical device, yet landlords were frequently able to persuade the courts of the need for it. One can scarcely conceive an act more disastrous or discouraging to hard-working farmers. To be forbidden entry to one's fields in the midst of the cultivating season was tantamount to loss of a crop. Indeed, such orders often meant the literal ruin of the tenant and the destruction of a potential food supply.

The process followed by landlords and the courts to pre-empt the legal responsibilities of the village commissions was uniquely Japanese. The first step in this process required that the tenant voluntarily

agree to return the rented land to the landlord. In what must have
been a weird conversation, the tenant simply surrendered his right to
cultivate the land. These strange transactions which violated all
western concepts of logic are yet another testimonial to the strength
of the landlord's traditional position. However it was really not
necessary to ask Tanaka-san to return the rented land. A landlord
could merely announce publicly in Tanaka-san's presence, say at
some social gathering, that as a fine example of old-fashioned Japanese courtesy and moral uprightness, Tanaka-san had already returned the land. Such was the power of the social sanctions that
Tanaka-san could not have contradicted the landlord's statement. So
in thousands of cases the landlords were able to force this vital initial
surrender.

The landlord then proceeded to the local court. There he presented
the case under the Tenant Arbitration Law of 1924, as a landlord-
tenant dispute voluntarily settled by mutual agreement. The court
formally recognized the agreement and gave the land to the landlord.
The court's decree was tantamount to dispossession notice. If the
tenant subsequently refused to accept the decision, he was automatically in contempt of court. Occasional resistance to the court's order
indicated the tenant's ignorance of the full implication of his initial
renunciation. Sometimes it meant that his initial consent had been
obtained by subterfuge. In other cases the landlord had proceeded on
the assumption that the initial step of securing renunciation was unnecessary. In any event, the courts made little or no effort to determine the actual facts. They felt that the landlord's account of the
matter was sufficient evidence and since it was unnecessary for the
tenant to be present in the court, there was no opportunity for his side
to be heard.

At this point one might have raised the question of the relation of
this procedure to the Land Reform Law. The courts had an answer:
"Fair enough," they said, "but the new law provides, under its Article
9, that the land commission has jurisdiction over landlord-tenant
agreements, where *a party* to the lease of agricultural lands intends
to terminate or rescind the lease. We interpret this to mean *a single
party*, without the consent of the other party. Hence your new law
does not cover the case in point, because here *both parties* to the
agreement have indicated their wish to terminate it... since your law
does not cover such cases your commission has no jurisdiction."

Under the rules of the game, as long as Japanese citizens obeyed
their own laws and their government endeavored to carry out Occupation directives, there was no basis for Occupation intervention. Landlord opposition had not overtly violated these ground rules except in
occasional instances. Yet it was inevitable that their camouflaged
resistance would, sooner or later, bring them into conflict with the
Occupation. Already it was the failure of vigorous investigation and
prosecution that had saved numbers of them from easy conviction.
Yet, as on so many other occasions, the Occupation waited and watched

for the opportune moment. Out in the prefectures and down in the villages, agricultural officers of Military Government were quietly but assiduously examining all available details of cases involving the dispossession of tenants. An imposing array of damaging facts was being assembled. Yet on the surface all was serene.

Finally detailed work by Military Government officers at the town of Utsunomiya, near Tokyo, unearthed the necessary incriminating case. In that town, the public prosecutor of a large judicial district had suppressed hundreds of official tenant complaints, varying from allegations of illegal eviction to charges of assault. This was flagrant dereliction of duty by an important official.

Under pressure, the Utsunomiya procurator gave the show away completely. He involved not only his own staff but numbers of landlords and local police officers. In the flurry of discovery, confession, and incrimination, local and district courts were just barely able to clear their skirts. As it was, they were considerably humbled. At last the Occupation was in position to press a charge of collusion by government officials to defeat an Occupation directive. The guilty could have been held to answer before an Occupation court and the Japanese Government could have been made to suffer great humiliation.

But a more effective course was followed. The Japanese were given the option of doing a thorough job of house cleaning among their recalcitrant and dilatory law enforcement personnel. In this crisis the Ministries of Agriculture and Forestry, Justice, and Home Affairs conferred with officials of the Supreme Court of Japan. The result was a mild, but effective, reminder, issued in the name of the Supreme Court, to all principal law enforcement officials in the country. This memorandum stated that the land reform statute was a law, to be respected as such. Particular emphasis was placed on the legality of land commissions and of their decisions. The court also called polite attention to those regions in which close attention should be paid to the new law. Effects of the message were immediate and widespread. Together with the notoriety of the Utsunomiya case, it was sufficient to reduce quickly the harrassment of tenants to negligible proportions.

Throughout this period of harrassment, the main concern of the Occupation and the Japanese Government was to keep the land commissions on the job. In spite of numerous diversionary attacks by landlord interests, the commissions were told to keep on working. They were to disregard slights to their dignity. These slights as well as evictions and temporary restraining orders were hard to bear, but since they were for the most part illegal, they could, in time, be corrected. What was indispensable was a sustained record of commission action. Nothing the landlords might plan could offset the cumulative effect of a sustained drive by the commissions. Hence it was essential that commissioners concentrate on their appointed task; everything else was of lesser importance. Tenants wanted, above everything else, a clear demonstration that the commissions could act and did have authority.

Further Attempts by Landlords to Block Reform

But the landlords were by no means routed by the Utsunomiya case and its aftermath. A first and important round had been lost and so had valuable allies. But they soon recovered and launched another, although more indirect, attack. In contrast to their earlier informal and haphazard organizations, they now developed a much more efficient grouping of local units into prefectural and regional confederacies. These federations took such names as the Autonomous Farmers Association, Farmers Cooperative Association, and the Farmland Problem Studying Society. They served as intelligence and strategy planning centers from which leaders were able to consolidate the dissidence of individual landlords into a concerted plan.

Leaders of these confederacies were sophisticated and well informed. They shunned all extra legal activities; rather, they relied on their ability to affect public opinion through the media of publicity. In fact, in the first year of the land transfer period, their influence with the press enabled them to present almost exclusively their side of the picture. For its part, the press seemed willing enough to slant the news in behalf of the landlords. On the other hand, almost the entire Japanese press, including the great metropolitan dailies, failed completely to do justice to the positive side of the reform program. Repeatedly these papers were given detailed, timely, and newsworthy stories. Almost invariably these were emasculated, buried in the back pages, omitted completely, or twisted in a fashion to create an unfavorable or negative impression.

In this second phase of attack, landlords concertedly played variations on the theme that land ownership was a burdensome responsibility. Tenants were told by their landlords that they were, after all, weary of the burden of land ownership. As a landowner one had to pay very heavy taxes and then one never knew what the taxes might be since the government was continually changing its mind. The tax might even be more than the value of the produce from the land. Tenants were sometimes told that the government was just waiting for the transfer to be accomplished before imposing terrific taxes on them. Again, landlords pointed to their own plight: If the government could force the landlord to sell his land now, what might it not later do to the tenant when he in turn had become a landowner? In some places this psychological attack did frighten the tenants. According to the Akita Military Government officers, "The tenants were not very enthusiastic over the chance to buy land because the landlords said they were glad to get rid of the burden and expense of land ownership."

Sometimes tenants were frightened into illegal collusive agreements. In one instance, several tenants joined a criminal conspiracy, persuaded by the argument that "even though you would happen to buy an agricultural land under the present farm land reform law, you can gain nothing from your purchased land because the government can take back your land under the land reform law at the same price you pay for it. But if you agree with us, in designating the whole area as town lots, we can sell them at a higher price and we will share the proceeds with you, giving you thirty or forty per cent of the sale price." Such tactics occasionally resulted also in the corruption of tenant members of Village Land Commissions.

It is difficult to assess the value of these attacks. True, tenants all over Japan continually mentioned the heavy responsibilities of land ownership in discussing the merits of the program. So they must have been impressed somewhat with the landlord propaganda. But after all, the real purpose of all landlord strategy was to slow down or stop the work of land commissions, and this purpose the whispering campaign was not able to accomplish. Landlord strategists then sought to link up this psychological weapon with a more direct and dramatic device.

This new device was a scheme to challenge the constitutionality of the Land Reform Law. Japan had put into effect a new democratic constitution on May 3, 1947. In the drafting of this document, Occupation legal specialists had been closely consulted and General MacArthur had formally endorsed the completed document. So the landlord strategists figured that they could create a maximum of public interest in their resistance program if they took a leaf out of the judicial history of the American New Deal period. Accordingly, cases challenging the constitutionality of the Land Reform Law were filed sporadically throughout Honshu, beginning in the summer of 1947 and continuing throughout the rest of the year. This was an integrated campaign directed by capable men, principal among whom was a former Minister of Justice.

The scheme had cleverness. In a sense it tied the Occupation's hands because of its formal endorsement of the Constitution. Hence an attack on the Land Reform Program in the name of the new constitution could not be interpreted as an attack on an Occupation objective. Logically it was an effort to test one set of principles in the light of another set; on the surface a highly intellectual undertaking. Yet the whole purpose of this new attack was again to discourage and confuse tenants. Of course this practical aim was carefully concealed behind high-flown phrases about democracy and the sacred rights of private property. It is very doubtful that the proponents of the plan had any intention of actually letting many of the cases which they filed come to trial. The principal purpose was to provide a springboard for publicity and anti-land reform agitation.

The litigation had the advantage of again invoking the awe-inspiring majesty of the judicial process without actually involving the court's integrity. Every step in the procedure, beginning with the initial filing of the cases, provided the occasion for developing an intensely political atmosphere. Inflammatory speeches were delivered. Brochures were published. Funds were solicited. A general atmosphere of gaudy display and excitement was fostered, although not always successfully. Newspapers gave full accounts of all the events attendant on the filing of the cases and their subsequent preparation. One special tactic was to announce that an impressive list of witnesses had been called to testify. These witnesses were selected more on account of the prestige of their names and the attendant publicity which could be created by their use than by any direct relation to agriculture or knowledge of land problems. In this fashion, the names of the Prime Minister, ex-Prime Ministers, heads of political parties, prominent scholars, and other great and near-great men were used.

The architects of this plan made special effort to insure that the impact of this uproar bore heavily on Joe Tanaka down in his village. They hoped that the invocation of all the pomp and circumstance which they had arranged would scare him. They wanted him to feel at once both the scope of the drama in which he was involved and the weight of his responsibility in bringing it all about. They arranged to see that he was continually reminded of the unorthodox role which he was playing. They saw to it that he was laughed at for his pretensions. They endeavored to surround all his goings and comings with a gentle neighborly scorn and a universal "see what you've done now, you rascal" atmosphere. All this was designed to bring Joe to an attitude of shame and humility in which he and all his fellow tenants would completely renounce all their rights under the new law. By creating a legal situation, involving the prestige of the courts, the opposition wanted to make Joe feel that he personally was being haled before the bar of justice as a quasi offender.

But always, and most important of all, they hoped to bring about the withdrawal of Joe Tanaka's support from the tenant members on the Village Land Commissions. If this could only be partially effective, they calculated it would increase the defeatism of the more timid commissioners and tend to slow up or halt the commissions' activities. They harped continually on the theme that all the commission activities would certainly go for naught when the court finally threw out the whole reform legislation as unconstitutional.

The psychological insight of the landlord leadership during this phase was excellent, but the timing was a little off. The original tenant psychology in March, 1947, at the start of the land transfer program was completely in line with methods used during the constitutionality campaign. But by the time that campaign got under way, the element of hope had been strengthened just enough among tenants to take the edge from its effect. If the campaign had started a little earlier, it might have had a better chance of success. As it was, the plan caused plenty of trouble. The first case was filed in Hokkaido, hearings were held on August 5, 1947, and a decision in favor of the government was rendered in September. By early October a considerable number of cases had been prepared and filed.

But in the meantime, and almost unexpectedly, the landlord cause received a sledge-hammer blow. Against a scheduled purchase on October 2, 1947, of 443,646 acres the land commissions reported the purchase from landlords of a tremendous 854,388 acres, an amount equal to more than the combined purchases of the previous March and

July. The combined total of lands acquired from landlords now reached the impressive total of 1,707,689 acres. Since on the average, an acre of farm land is composed of about six tiny parcels, the government's acquisitions amounted to more than ten million of these parcels. Thus almost certainly some land had been purchased in every village in Japan. Almost as significant as the splendid purchase accomplishment was the simultaneous transfer of over 200,000 acres of land into the possession of tenants. This was the first actual fruit of the reform in terms of the practical calculations of tenants. In terms of parcels of land this figure meant that not less than a quarter of a million tenant families benefited from this initial distribution.

Indeed things were moving! Everywhere in Japan a great new force was slowly stirring. Not in their full stride yet, nor with any certainty, but stumblingly, haltingly, the farm tenants of Japan were beginning to behave like free men. Here was the slow moving force for which the planners of land reform had been waiting.

Chapter 12

LAND REFORM
AND THE JAPANESE GOVERNMENT

W HILE knotty problems were posed by the landlord opposition,
difficulties almost as serious arose within the Japanese government. Of course the government's efficiency had been
greatly impaired by the war and by the postwar deficiencies. Yet it
was the inherent character of government itself that caused the most
stubborn problems. This government had been developed for the purpose of carrying out an autocratic and imperial purpose. But now this
administrative structure was attempting to achieve a democratic purpose. Unfortunately, government machinery conforms to the ends it
serves. When these ends of government are the maintenance of a
caste system, it is difficult for the corresponding mechanism to adapt
itself to duties derived from democratic principles.

Because of the need for insuring uniformity of action and policy,
and because of the uncertainty of local finances, it had been planned
that the financial needs of the village commissions would be defrayed
by disbursements from the central government. Thus the commissions had been encouraged to go ahead with their work on the assurance that they would be paid by the government. These payments
were essential to defray commission expense of which the most important item was the salaries of commission clerks.

These clerks were indispensable. They were the administrative
and executive arm of the commission system. They gave continuity
and force to commission decisions. But the salary arrangement assumed that the central government could reverse its role as a revenue collector and become a fiscal disbursing agent. Experience soon
proved that the entire government housekeeping procedures were so
entangled with tradition, and so entrenched, that it accomplished these
new duties with utmost awkwardness. Indeed, the channels of Japanese government finance were one-way passages, and traffic which
did not move toward Tokyo moved always upstream, against an adverse bureaucratic current.

It was all very well to lay plans which called for the movement of
funds out of Tokyo. But it was another matter to encounter the crosscurrents of rank prerogatives within the government itself. It was
clear that the Japanese government ultimately must make funds available to the commissions. But this commitment did not alter the fact

that the Minister of Finance outranked considerably the somewhat
junior Minister of Agriculture. Therefore, in bureaucratic eyes it
was completely inappropriate that requisitions for funds to defray
commission expenses transmitted to Finance by Agriculture carried
the implication of a demand. But since the disbursements must be
made to conform to an Occupation principle, it could not be ultimately
denied. Thus the traditional role of the two Ministers was reversed.

The Finance Ministry simply acted as though the request was fully
within its power to accept or reject. Finance officials insisted on
their privilege of completely reviewing all details of these budgets.
They made independent judgments as to the merits of the amounts of
salaries paid to individual clerks as well as the items of commission
expense. These officials presumed to determine when and in what
amounts disbursements should be made to the commissions. This
procedure of course took them into the details of the Land Reform Law
itself which they studied at length. When challenged, these lengthy
steps were all justified on the grounds that the Finance Minister was
after all the watchdog of the Treasury.

On such grounds these financiers intruded into the operations of
land reform where they had no real business. They forced endless
wranglings as to the way in which the program was being administered.
They wanted to know why it could not be administered in some other
way. They seemed to delight in holding up certifications of the most
sorely needed funds because of minute discrepancies. By such means
the Minister of Agriculture and his staff were made to remember that
although their requests might have the color of an order because they
originated from a GHQ-sponsored program, yet actually the traditional relation remained fully in effect – "and don't you forget it."

This petty bureaucratic byplay was damaging. In the tiny village of
Sekimoto, some sixty miles north of Tokyo, we spent some time with
the pleasant young secretary of the local land commission in the early
fall of 1947. As we conversed, in the dingy dimness of the village
office, it became plain that he had done an outstanding job. He spoke
enthusiastically of his commission's progress and of the good which
the program would do in his village. Yet the boy's personal story was
pathetic. His office supplies had been exhausted for weeks. He was
harassed by impatient creditors to whom the commission was indebted
for a variety of services. A married man with several children and
no resources save his tiny salary, he had been unpaid for several
months. His anxiety and uncertainty increased as repeated inquiries
about his salary remained unanswered. Soon in desperation he would
have to quit and the land reform program would be the loser.

Investigation of similar cases disclosed that the central government had devised an incredibly cumbersome method for transmitting
money to the villages. Funds passed through checkpoint after checkpoint at each of which elaborate records were maintained. At almost
every one of these points the squabble between Finance and Agriculture
was fought all over again. As the funds reached successively lower

stages in their time-consuming journey, an elaborate system of counterfoils was maintained. One copy of the counterfoil went back to Tokyo, another went to the last checkpoint, another to the next checkpoint, and still another to the point of destination. All this meant that a voucher on its way to a distant village was weeks, if not months, in transit.

A number of commission clerks were forced to abandon their jobs because of poverty. Others quit in disgust. A few took bribes. Sometimes lack of funds compelled an entire commission to suspend operations. The dereliction of the Tamagawa Land Commission near Tokyo probably had its origin in financial difficulties. This commission started by charging unauthorized fees to defray its unpaid expenses. This soon proved profitable. The commission's income grew to three times its official budget. Then the commission offered its services, at a price, to help convert agricultural land into nonagricultural land. Finally individual commissioners sold their individual services as "mediators" with the commission.

In October, 1947, the situation had reached a crisis. Occupation officials called in the Ministers of Agriculture and of Finance and sternly advised them that the game of rank would not be permitted to interfere with the program. For a while the Minister of Finance became more cooperative and devised a more realistic and much faster system for handling funds. With these innovations, the situation in most villages had greatly improved by the first of the year. But the fundamental contradictions continued to operate so that by the spring of 1948, distress among the villages was so great that, as an emergency measure, prefectural officials were authorized to borrow at local branches of the Bank of Japan to cover current deficits.

Readers perhaps will wonder why the local community was not taxed to support the commissions. In the first place, landlords might have refused to pay such a tax and with some justification. Secondly, there was a real danger that the tax could have been used as a device to intimidate tenants. Thirdly, the collection and disbursement of such a tax would have placed great power in the traditional village officials and the *buraku* leaders. At the very least, such a procedure would have enabled each village to exercise a great deal of discretion as to just how the reform should be conducted with a resultant lack of uniformity in the program. On the other hand, as long as the central government controlled the purse, it was in a position to require standards of performance and continuity.

Change in Land Transfer Policy

In spite of handicaps, the outcome of the December 31, 1947, land transfer was very satisfactory. New purchases from landlords on that date accounted for 1,155,508 acres and sales to tenants amounted to 224,871 acres. Cumulative progress was reflected in totals of all land purchased at 2,863,197 acres and total sales to tenants of 448,718 acres. Some prefectures were nearing the goals set for them by the central government. Indeed a number of villages were on the point of declaring that they had completed the appointed task. This difficulty was created basically because of inadequate and inaccurate government data. The government simply didn't know how much land there was; consequently, its quotas were little more than guesses. Yet from a morale standpoint it would be disastrous to encourage a prefecture and its component villages to work against a quota when achievement of the quota meant an incomplete program.

Throughout the civilian departments of Japanese government, statistics were frequently inaccurate and unreliable. To many Japanese the difference between a lot and a little is an adequate measuring stick. So the quotas which had been calculated on the basis of census material proved to be useful only in the earlier months of the program. Continued use of these quotas as tools of administration would have caused a partial failure of the program, as check of several villages which were about to fulfil their official quotas disclosed.

So it was necessary to formulate a new policy and place it in effect. Prefectures were ordered to instruct all villages that the quotas were withdrawn. There was to be no statistical stopping place on the road to complete reform. Instead, purchases were to continue until no land legally eligible for purchase remained. When this task had been achieved, it was to be verified by an official inspection. Actually, this latter scrutiny turned out to be hardly necessary for, as the tenant commissioners gained confidence, they eagerly searched out the last tiny bit of land which they deemed eligible for purchase.

The quota and goal system was terminated none too soon, because, as the commissions delved deeper and deeper into the program, their problems became increasingly difficult and complex. Thus under the quota arrangement there would have been an incentive to halt the program short of completion because of the increasingly hard work involved. Again it should be pointed out that the deficiency of the quota system represented another bureaucratic shortcoming at the village level, where bureaucratic deadlocks sometimes caused almost complete frustration of the local commissions.

Problem of Tax Lands

One of the most annoying of these conflicts arose in regard to so-called *tax lands*. These were agricultural lands acquired by the government, through the Ministry of Finance, from owners who had petitioned the tax authorities to take their land at its tax valuation as payment of taxes. Frequently tax payers found this expedient an attractive way of meeting the very heavy postwar property taxes. It was easier for them to hand the land over to the tax authorities than to find the necessary cash to pay the tax. Since land could not increase in value, while other assets might, it was possible to dispose of land at a comparative advantage, particularly if the land was eligible for transfer under the Land Reform Law.

Lands transferred to the government in this fashion went into the custody of the district officials of the Finance Ministry. Upon receipt of such lands, these tycoons of Japanese bureaucracy were then supposed to transfer it to the Village Land Commissions for sale to tenants. But instead of developing a smooth technique for handling the transfers, the two ministries proceeded to manufacture an almost incredible muddle.

For over a year after the inauguration of the land reform program, the records of the Finance Ministry were in such bad shape that it was almost impossible to determine just which lands had passed into their custody via the tax route. This uncertainty added to the land commissions' burdens and created general confusion. For example, after lengthy debate a village commission would perhaps choose a number of tracts for a particular purchase plan. According to all the village records, these tracts were properly eligible for purchase. But frequently, after a great deal of work and after the purchase plan had been approved, it would be discovered that the land already belonged to the government as tax lands. One or two experiences of this sort made the village commissioners feel that they were being imposed on; much worse, that they had been made to look foolish.

It seemed a simple remedy to have the local Finance offices notify the villages of all the lands which had been turned over to them as payments in lieu of taxes. But such a simple remedy failed to consider bureaucratic prerogatives. The Finance people regarded tax records as their special business. They felt no obligation whatever to share their lofty concerns with the lowly agencies of local government. So they insisted that the status of a particular piece of land could not be determined until after the commission had acted. In fact, they refused to let the local commissioners complete transfers for land which they might later decide to take over for taxes.

In the general conduct of land transfer operations, the very fact that the land was already in the government's possession was in itself misleading. It caused miscalculations as to the amount of land the government could transfer to tenants at any given time. In the earlier months of the reform this situation was almost disastrous because everyone assumed that, with the land already in the government's possession, there remained only the job of selling it to the tenants. Therefore it was logical to place such lands in the government land inventory along with lands purchased under the Land Reform Law. The assumption was that the Finance people would immediately transfer their land inventory to Agriculture which would then notify the commissions to dispose of the land to the tenants. But instead, each agency jealously guarded its ancient prerogatives, with the result that land in the possession of the Finance Ministry seemed more inaccessible to tenants than ever before.

Still more confusing, the inventory of land held by the tax offices was continually shifting as additional land-owners offered their land in lieu of taxes. Sometimes landlords were negotiating with tax officials to take over their land concurrently with commission action to purchase the land under the land reform law. In July, 1947, when the Ministry of Agriculture reported that it had acquired through purchase 853,301 acres, the Finance Ministry holdings were reported at 624,870 acres. From these two reports it appeared at first sight that the total government land inventory was 1,378,171 acres. If this estimate had been correct, it would have represented great progress. The unwary could have dismissed the actual poor showing of the commissions in contemplating the apparent substantial government holdings.

The governor of Niigata prefecture counted so heavily on the availability of tax lands for transfer purposes that no efforts were made in that prefecture to prosecute purchases under the Land Reform Law until the late summer of 1947. Unfortunately the Finance Ministry figures turned out to be grossly inaccurate. They were officially revised sharply downward in November, 1947, and by mid-1948 the figure had shrunk to 425,065 acres. The amount of time spent in reconciling the discrepancies was fantastic. Finally, as in so many other cases, the problem was solved by the tedious process of "sweating it out." Time and patient effort reduced the confusion to negligible proportions. But similar difficulties were encountered in all the other categories of government-owned lands which were technically eligible for early transfer to tenants.

Problem of Former Military Land

During the war Japanese military commanders had taken farm land for camp sites, maneuver areas, airfields, bombing ranges, etc. Residents were abruptly and unceremoniously moved off, and accounts were to be settled at the end of the war. In this manner, large amounts of land passed into military custody. After surrender, this property, termed *former military land,* passed into the jurisdiction of the Occupation and was almost immediately handed back to the Japanese government to be distributed in accordance with the Land Reform Law. The administration of this property constituted another set of difficult problems.

The lands were scattered all over Japan and records of their location and original ownership were inaccurate and confused. Many of the original owners of these fields had disappeared in the upheaval of the war. In other cases it was impossible to trace former ownership lines, especially as the conversion of the original farms to military use had completely obliterated original agricultural features; moreover, reconversion to tillage was in many instances an arduous and expensive task. Since the government had many more immediate tasks, its administration of such lands drifted on a haphazard course. In a number of cases these properties and what remained of the original military structures became a haven for all sorts of squatters. In some instances, the original Japanese military organization having

wartime jurisdiction simply remained in occupancy. Of course these
military personnel "put their hats on backward" to make it appear
that they were genuine farmers.

In Ibaraki prefecture, a flagrant example of seizing ownerless land
occurred. Motonao Samejima, a former captain in the Japanese navy
and his naval associates set up what they called Tsukuba Free Farm
on the site of the 588-acre Yatabe Naval Air Base. The group consisted of nearly fifty people, seven of whom were former naval officers and another twenty who were former naval enlisted men. In view
of the strict demands of the allies for the abolition of every trace of
militarism and the unequivocal return to civilian life of all military
personnel, this pre-emption bordered on defiance of the Occupation.
According to reports received by GHQ, the group maintained regular
military form and discipline. Work was performed on the orders of
the commissioned staff; duties were apportioned according to rank;
and quarters, privileges, and facilities were similarly allocated.

Even in terms of Japanese law the whole undertaking was flagrantly
illegal; ex-Captain Samejima had not the slightest claim to the use of
the property. His presence and that of his colleagues on the air base
lands was simply trespass. But these violations were only the start.
The bold Captain next negotiated a loan of ¥1,200,000 with Banno
Busan Products Ltd., a Tokyo commercial firm. Under the terms of
the loan, Tsukuba Farm became the agricultural department of the
Banno concern and the proceeds of the loan were used as working
capital and for the purchase of heavy mechanized equipment.

A more radical violation of law and policy could hardly be conceived. Yet Captain Samejima and his associates got away with their
scheme for quite some time. Their very boldness seemed almost to
stun the Japanese government. One almost did a "double take" only
to find that the facts remained the same, and just as big as life. Yet
all the while Samejima and his associates composedly went about their
business completely ignoring the Occupation, the Japanese government,
and the Village Land Commission.

Perhaps the most significant aspect of the matter was the hesi-
tance and delay of the Japanese government in dealing with it. The
matter first came to official attention in February, 1947. Yet, in
spite of the factual issues involved, it took the government over two
years of continual fussy exertion to bring the farce to an end. This
was only one instance of the government's efforts to administer the
474,500 acres of this former military land.

Another instance of long-deferred government action on lands in a
somewhat different category arose in connection with *Suehiro* (The
Folding Fan) Farm in Chiba prefecture. This 490-acre estate of the
famous Mitsubishi family remained exempt from land reform for
months. Perhaps because the Mitsubishi family was traditionally so
powerful, the local village commission hesitated to apply the Land
Reform Law. The owners cleverly avoided any overt action to evade
the law. But somehow they persuaded the great Kirin Beer Brewery

Company to use some of the Suehiro land for the experimental cultivation of barley. Now the Kirin Company occasionally sold beer to the 8th U. S. Army for its enlisted and officer clubs. This seemed to the Suehiro people a close enough official connection with the Allied Occupation to justify posting the property with signs reading "The Supplying Farm for the 8th Army Designated Plant" and "The Experiment Farm for the 8th Army Designated Plant." The signs didn't say "keep off" or "no trespassing" but they implied prohibition.

The local land commissions, of course, gained the impression that the property had been put under Occupation protection and was not subject to the Land Reform Law. More sophisticated prefectural officials, who could not be taken in by this deception, were beguiled by the Suehiro management with the idea of converting the entire farm into an experimental farm. It was claimed that, in this fashion, although the ownership might remain in the Mitsubishi family, still the whole nation would benefit far more than through subdivision and sale to tenants. So the farm continued to operate as a country estate while prefectural officials drew up fanciful schemes for research into animal breeding, in spite of the fact that Japan already had more of these experimental farms than it could possibly support. After months of wrangling, and at the insistence of the Occupation, the central government finally intervened and brought the farm under the law.

Another Zaibatsu family, the Mitsui, owned a dairy farm near Tokyo. Farmers in the neighborhood complained that this farm had escaped the Land Reform Law. They pointed out that their own average holdings were less than one acre – why should the Mitsui continue to own 18 acres? They argued that they were compelled to turn over a large portion of their production to the national crop collection system, while the 18-acre Mitsui dairy produced milk and dairy products only for the Mitsui, their employees, and friends. Such a condition, the farmers asserted, was "unreasonable cultivation" within the meaning of the Land Reform Law which required that all production must conform to the food requirements of the total population. The farmers were quite right. Yet in spite of perfectly plain facts, the Government was not able to conclude its investigation of the Mitsui farm until June, 1948, although the initial complaint was made early in 1947.

An important aspect of these delays was the adverse effect on farmer morale. The rural people viewed the effectiveness of government action as an indicator of the government's sincerity in pushing the program. It was all very well for the government to urge the land commissions to undertake a serious personal responsibility. But the farmers wanted to know what the government people themselves were willing to do. Were they really willing to challenge powerful interests and bold individuals? If the government hesitated to take appropriate action, then how could it expect humble peasants to undertake such risks?

The "Pasture Land" Dispute

In its transition from an instrumentality of Imperial policy to an instrument for administering democratically enacted laws, the Japanese government was called on to accept the burden of final administrative responsibility. Its officials had to learn how to make decisions. At times, this responsibility was a cruel burden and there was a great temptation to shift it to the shoulders of others. For this reason, Occupation officials had to be continually on guard against accepting responsibility which properly was not theirs. But Occupation people had to learn to accept conditions which existed in Japan as a framework within which their own objectives must be accomplished. This entailed the hard lesson that they had to expend a great deal more energy to get a single act of responsibility discharged by the Japanese than a similar job would entail if performed directly.

For instance, in the summer of 1947 a glaring deficiency in the language of the Land Reform Law came to light. This deficiency hinged on the meaning of the single word *cultivated*. If the word did not include lands used for animal husbandry, then a very large and important acreage on the northernmost island of Hokkaido was excluded from the Land Reform Law. The Americans found themselves embroiled in an interminable legal argument. Finally it developed that the law did not include animal husbandry lands, making it necessary to amend the law in order to bring this type of land into the reform program. If this amendment were not made, then the land reform in Hokkaido would fail widely of effectiveness.

Hokkaido is the northernmost and largest of the four Japanese islands. It lies close to Soviet territory, and from the Siberian mainland the chilly winds of climate and politics give the island a unique climate and significance among the Japanese islands. For well over a century, the Japanese have sought to exploit Hokkaido's economic potential. But even today it is a frontier. While much of it has been subdued, there still remain large stretches of forests and bog where a few semi-destitute settlers wrest a hazardous existence from poor soil and an inhospitable climate. At the same time, more cultivable sections exhibit the same pattern of tenancy as do the other islands. But the pattern is not uniform. Large areas of good cultivable land are used inefficiently for pastures and grazing areas of estates which, in organization and character, constitute a distinct type of farm enterprise.

The Occupation became aware of the Hokkaido situation only gradually. As the pattern of great Hokkaido estates and the wretched condition of the villagers on these many estates became clearer, it also became clear that a peculiar type of feudalism flourished there untouched by the reforms of the three more southerly islands. Moreover, it was apparent that the tenant situation which prevailed on these estates certainly required the application of the principle of land reform as much or more than in the case of any other agricultural lands.

It was difficult to find out much about Hokkaido. A puzzling feature was the large number of government-owned horse breeding establishments. Although it was never proved, a strong suspicion remained that in times past these breeding farms had been a remount service for the military. The big estates were almost impenetrable by motor vehicle. Yet the farmsteads, when one finally reached them, after hours of uncomfortable travel on very bad roads, seemed remarkably modern in contrast to the primitive transportation conditions. Some of these estates were owned by absentees who resided in the large cities and visited the farms only rarely. Other estates were owned by corporations whose stockholders were difficult to trace. On some of the estates one found primitive villages whose people had some cloudy indeterminate relation to the estate. Inquiries about the whole situation developed disappointingly few concrete facts. Nevertheless, the available information did vaguely depict a sort of Japanese East Prussia supporting a semi-military caste system somewhat on the order of the Junkers.

At any rate, a large portion of the Japanese livestock industry was concentrated on these estates. Yet the lands were not efficiently used. Actually the concentration of the lands in the hands of a largely absentee and corporate ownership made the development of a real livestock industry almost impossible.

At first, Ministry officials sought to explain the original exclusion of these lands as a trifling legal oversight. This was not so certain because as a result of the discussions concerning amendment of the law, word soon got to the powerful livestock interests that their lands might be included in the reform. They responded with a vigorous lobbying pressure directed at government officials. Several government officials then sought to persuade the Occupation that it would be a severe blow to Japanese animal husbandry if the reform were applied to these Hokkaido estates. When this argument was refuted by Occupation livestock experts, the next argument was that the problem of subdividing the estates was technically too difficult. Next followed several abortive attempts to influence directly the views of individual members of the Occupation. These various pressure-group activities raised a suspicion that the original omission of these estates from the Land Reform Law had not been inadvertent.

Finally, at the end of December, 1947, the law was amended. The amendments were carefully drawn to protect all legitimate and special features of Japanese animal husbandry. This much accomplished, the problem of enforcing the new provisions had to be faced. Enforcement turned out to be a major undertaking. Here again, inaccuracy, hesitation, and vacillation of a civil government unaccustomed to exercise final administrative authority, were principal stumbling blocks to progress. The result was a delay until mid-1949 of the completion of the pasture land acquisition program.

Further Governmental Problems

While the "pasture land" dispute placed a heavy burden on the personnel of the Ministry of Agriculture, still another controversy was developing. This was an interminable, bitter wrangle to decide which land was actually farm land and which was urban real estate. Originally this problem arose from the cultivation of city lands which had been devastated by fire and bombing. These areas were former residential and industrial sites which war's destruction had converted into open fields and thus had been promptly placed under cultivation by a variety of squatters. In addition to this type of land, there were parks, playgrounds, golf courses, and green belts which had been placed under cultivation in a more controlled fashion as part of the war effort. Since no one interfered, the cultivators of both kinds of land came to feel they had special status. Eventually they claimed that this property should be considered subject to the Land Reform Law. Simultaneously, reconstruction and war-sufferer relief projects caused city authorities to develop programs involving not only bombed areas but adjacent farm fields.

The row that developed was monumental. Timid land commissions, completely in awe of the landlords, seemed to have no fear of their urban neighbors. Perhaps it was because in attempting to seize urban lands they found a temporary escape from the emotional tensions which accompanied disputes with their feudal superiors. No such inhibitions bothered them in precipitating quarrels with urban people. At any rate, several commissions vigorously pressed completely phony claims to urban lands. But then, the city planning officials and other urban authorities seemed to have little regard for rural rights or feelings. In turn, they staked out areas of valuable farm land as sites for housing projects, schools, or insane asylums. This type of planning offered landlords a splendid escape route. In some instances, landlords literally begged city planners to include their farm lands in urban reconstruction schemes. Of course if this could be accomplished, agricultural land became city land, no longer subject to the land reform law. Such converted land could be sold by the owner at any price the buyer cared to pay, or held by the original owner as a very desirable investment.

The din and clamor which these arguments created involved city officials, urban labor leaders, land commissions, and educational and religious groups. There seemed to be no beginning and no end to the conflict. Rulings by the central government were either disregarded or vigorously questioned by one or several of the interested parties. What seemed often to be final settlements turned out to be only incidents in the long embittered brawls.

One of the satellite towns of the Kobe-Osaka industrial complex contained a 50-acre tract. Part of this tract was a former factory site which had been destroyed by bombs. Adjacent to it was an unfinished real estate subdivision intended for factory-worker homes.

During the war, the subdivision scheme had been temporarily aban-
doned. In the interval, the factory workers in the neighborhood had
become unemployed and so undertook to cultivate the vacant land.
When the legal owners appeared at the end of the war, the squatters
claimed to be tenant farmers and sought the protection of the Land
Reform Law against their "landlords." With no shadow of legal claim
to the lands, these squatters, by filling the air with outcries, were
able to create the semblance of a case. They forced the authorities
to hold hearings. At one of these sessions the testimony of the squatters was little more than ludicrous, bare-faced prevarication. The
descriptions of the land by these "tenants" heightened the comic
effect. One described his rights as including the factory assembly
yard. Another claimed as his fields "the roadway." Still another
thought that he should have the "recreation area." A land commission in a nearby village backed up these claims and the Prefectural
Land Commission and the governor agreed. The mayor of the city and
the city government of Osaka opposed the claim. Different parts of
the central government decided both for and against the squatters.

In most instances, these squabbles fell to the ground by their own
absurdity. Others had to be cured by definitive government action.
Fortunately, a general improvement in industrial employment conditions sent a number of the erstwhile agriculturalists back to their
normal employment. But the situation, which lasted for over two
years, underlined once more the comparative inability of the agencies
of civil government to deal effectively with situations in which they
were called upon to take action and to assume responsibility.

So the Government's traditions and historical perspective acted as
a drag on the progress of the reform. All problems which required
solution by collaboration with local communities and groups became
extraordinarily complex. Government coordination was never good
and its timing was always off. In the case of the very important information program which was planned to assist the farmers to understand the land reform program, lack of planning and coordination resulted in an almost complete failure. Perhaps the most disappointing
failure occurred in connection with the *kamishibai* episode.

Kamishibai literally means "paper theatre." So a *kamishibai* is a
sort of Japanese Punch and Judy show. Everywhere in the rural villages, when a small group of passers-by can be persuaded to spend a
half hour or so in amusement, one is apt to see the *kamishibai* man
practising his art — usually before a rapt juvenile audience. It's all
very simple — the impresario begins his tale, we suppose, in the
familiar "once upon a time" vein. As he talks, he draws from a small
case, one after another, gaudily colored twelve-by-fifteen-inch picture
cards and displays them on a tripod-supported stand. These are the
illustrations of the story he tells. His art consists in properly manip-
ulating the story and the pictures so that each picture is shown at the
most psychologically effective moment. Each performance takes about
half an hour and there are about fifteen pictures for each; then a

collection is taken up. Finally the *kamishibai* man packs up his props, mounts his bicycle, and is off in search of another audience. His stories are drawn from the vast storehouse of Japanese legends and myths, like the story of *Momotaro* (Little Peachling), a sort of Japanese Jack and the Beanstalk. There are other stories about the *Tengu* goblins with long red noses who fan themselves with leaves from the *Yatsuda* tree, or tales of the *Kappa,* a fantastic frog-like river boy — perhaps a Japanese waterbaby! For older audiences there are simplified versions of the legend of the 47 ronin and Lord Asano.

The value of the indigenous *kamishibai* as an information media for publicizing the land reform program was self-evident. Information specialists in GHQ suggested to the Japanese that the possibilities of the *kamishibai* device be explored. The Japanese, too, became enthusiastic. Eventually three separate stories about the land reform program were adapted for *kamishibai* production.

Nevertheless, the whole project failed. It failed because the Japanese government machinery was simply too inflexible to carry out in one combined operation the various steps and details of what seemed to the Americans a rather simple undertaking. And here again the interference of the Finance Minister was decisive. One gained the impression that down underneath, the dignified men of Finance were shocked at the very idea of an august and sacrosanct Japanese Government dealing in theatricals. Anyway, the Finance people insisted on their prerogative to demand a detailed description of every item of the *kamishibai* proposal. They objected at various points; they presumed to criticize artistic details although they knew nothing of art, drama, or educational techniques; they withheld funds; they withheld approval of the necessary permits to requisition paper which was rationed; and finally, they utterly rejected the idea of placing *kamishibai* men on the government payroll. Yet somehow an answer and a solution to all these objections was found.

After these obstacles had been overcome, there remained the problem of selecting the actual stories and illustrations. Again these were the subject of endless official debate. So the final product was gaudily inappropriate, completely lacking in charm or appeal. All the native delicacy and taste of unself-conscious Japanese art was lost in the deliberate striving for an effect. If the whole matter of producing the *kamishibai* was a frustrating experience, the simple matter of reproducing and distributing the several *kamishibai* sets was a nightmare. And the preparation of itineraries was still worse. Finally it became apparent that the coordination of official village sponsorship, distribution, and shipping of the *kamishibai* sets, and the scheduled itineraries, simply could not be achieved. In the end, the entire project was dropped after one or two abortive showings.

A somewhat similar fate befell many of the other informational and educational projects. Posters which took weeks to prepare were delivered only after the particular phase of the program they illustrated was no longer significant. Enormous amounts of effort went into the writing of handbooks and pamphlets intended for wide distribution. Yet it often turned out that the paper shortage permitted publication of only one copy per village and sometimes even less.

This experience in the face of the undoubted success of the land reform program leads to the conclusion that somehow the farmers of Japan carried on the program with almost none of the informational and educational guides which should have been indispensable. While there were numerous radio programs, no one could assess their value in view of the continual power failures, the poor repair of many sets, and the prevalent ignorance among bureaucrats of rural listener interests. Public lectures and discussions were undoubtedly effective. But their scope and influence were limited to the immediate community in which they took place. So for most of the rural areas of Japan, it was the overworked, underpaid land commission clerks who carried the burden of first instructing the commissioners and later of informing the cultivators as to the meaning of the Land Reform Law.

However, the government's ineptness for developing educational techniques for individual enlightment was sometimes offset to a degree by its capacity in developing enthusiasm and emulation among *groups*. One effective technique was the so-called *Mohanmura* (Model Village) system. These *Mohanmura* were frequently selected to demonstrate to groups from neighboring villages specific phases of the program. Perhaps one reason for the success of this method was its enhancement of the prestige of local authority. Headmen and lesser officials of the model village responded enthusiastically to this opportunity of basking in glory. Ceremonious greetings were exchanged with groups of visiting officials who were perhaps torn between jealousy of the honors bestowed on the rival village and a vivid mistrust of the reform itself.

But this experience also provided an opportunity for tenant commissioners to learn, from the tenant commissioners of the model village, methods for overcoming the problems of land reform in their own villages. In this way, a sense of tenant solidarity and responsibility was built up across village lines. It cannot be denied that the system was an effective as well as a quick and simple device for stimulating group action.

Another very successful technique was official recognition of exceptional performance. Here again the symbolism of authority was an important stimulus. November 23, 1947, the second anniversary of the original official announcement of the land reform program, was declared by the government a special national land reform memorial day.

The day was heralded by considerable publicity; ceremonies were held in all prefectural capitals; the Minister of Agriculture spoke over a national radio hookup and 110 bashful local land commissions received public commendation for outstanding efforts. More splendid still was the gift of a bicycle as an official gift to each of the 110 outstanding commissions. This last item symbolized perfectly the psychology of the occasion. Ten men received one bicycle. Not individual, but group recognition; not individual congratulation from one's fellow citizens, but group commendation from above, were the accepted symbols of successful performance.

These descriptions of the Japanese government's struggles to execute this great reform are not intended as blame. Rather, it is intended to portray the difficulties encountered by a government in attempting to achieve democratic goals. It is in part an account of government in transition. The men who carried the heavy responsibilities of the land reform program were the products of an autocratic government whose administrative structure was insensitive and unresponsive to the needs of its citizens; it lacked flexibility and was geared to only one speed and moved in only one direction. Too frequently the people who served this mechanism were shaped by its discipline. They, too, tended to become inflexible — unable to adapt government to the requirements of the governed.

To a very large degree, the emergence of a truly democratic Japan will depend on the success of the citizenry to bring the enormous bureaucracy of the Japanese government to an attitude of real public service. The people must teach the government new duties and new attitudes, particularly responsiveness to public demands and needs. It is worth emphasizing that many individuals in the Japanese Government strongly favored the land reform program. These men deserve commendation. But many of them lived through periods of frustration and despair for achievements which should not have been so costly in terms of effort and strain.

Chapter 13

SUCCESSES AND FAILURES

IN 1948 with the coming of summer a slight return of hope and confidence was discernible in the rural villages. A simple indicator was the reappearance of dogs. As they frisked in the streets and alleys, one recalled their former absence and reflected that perhaps a starving population cannot afford dogs. Children, too, seemed more lively and better fed.

As for land reform, the initial fears which it had brought to the villages were wearing off. Landlords, if not reconciled, were at least becoming accustomed to it. Tenants had lost a little of their dread of landlord reprisals and of village scorn as these failed to materialize or were halted by official action. Most land commissioners were now thoroughly experienced in the performance of their official duties and as a result, could accomplish more work with less time and effort.

In other segments of the economy, also, a slight improvement was becoming evident as one part after another of the wrecked and stalled production machinery began to move, albeit haltingly and uncertainly. Even this small revival had repercussions everywhere. Scant increments of chemical fertilizer were a boon to starved fields. Removal of a few items from strict rationing and the appearance at rare intervals of very limited stocks of petty luxuries were comforting. So, as renewed activities in mines, fisheries, and hydroelectric plants became even barely apparent, one could at least look toward a future, where before there had been no future. Finally there was clear evidence of the firm intent of the United States to continue its economic and political support of Japan. In the sharpening conflict between the Western world and the Soviet Union it was reassuring to the Japanese to know that their position was assured of protection.

Perhaps because of these psychological factors, perhaps only because of increased efficiency from familiarity and repetition, the July 2, 1948, land transfers broke all previous records. Combined purchases and sales of one and three quarters million acres on that date was the largest single land transfer in the entire program. With 18 months of the allotted 24 months elapsed, the cumulative totals were 5,423,386 acres taken from landlords and 1,865,957 acres transferred to tenants. These figures represented cultivated lands only. Pasture land transfers because of their different nature and because of the delay in settling that problem, were reported separately. This

achievement signified, as one Japanese put it, "that the backbone of
the problem of land transfers is now broken. What remains is the
prompt execution of details."

With the passing of the July transfer date, it became clear that the
commissions would come very close to meeting the land transfer assignment by the end of 1948. So for the first time in 18 months, the
commissioners could relax a little, confident in their ability to meet
all remaining challenges. Harassment, uncertainty, and strife were
of the past. Commissioners collectively and individually had won
their spurs as responsible public officials and they knew it. In this
new professional pride, tenants and landlord commissioners alike
could forget a little of their age-old feudal situation in a relationship
based on mutual achievement. Memories of inferiority and superiority were replaced by the reality of the recent common experience.
Many of these men now took pride in being addressed as Land Commissioner! Indeed, both in their own eyes and in those of their fellow
villagers, this title began to replace the former status designations of
tenant and lord of the land. In this way, a new dignity and standing
emerged, quite separate from the traditional village values.

Thus it was that in the first fortnight of July, 1948, village after
village celebrated the colorful *O-Bon* festival (Feast of the Dead) with
a sense of peace and serenity for the first time in many years. Food
for the festival was a little more plentiful. A more ample fertilizer
distribution gave assurance of better crops. A more stable electric
supply meant better lighted homes and longer, brighter evenings.

In these days, Tanaka-san, the tenant commissioner, could enjoy
himself for a few moments in the commission rooms at the village
office after a tiresome commission session. He might even sip a
little tea in amicable gossip with his brother commissioners. In this
place he now felt more comfortable. No longer was he so fearful or
ill at ease in the presence of the landlord commissioners. The portraits of the village dignitaries on the wall no longer implied to him
quite such an impassable social gulf. His very presence in the place
was far more significant, for the moment, than the social implications
of his origin.

Afterwards, as Land Commissioner Tanaka walked with his family
through the streets in the *O-Bon* rites to the ancestral graves, there
was an unconscious blending of the old and the new. On this Japanese
All Souls' Day, the ancestral spirits are guided by the living relatives
through evening shadows to their old homes. Lanterns are placed on
the graves and the families take care to light the return journey so
that all unsafe places may be avoided. Then in the home a meal is
prepared and the family gathers to converse with the returned spirits.
We may suppose that Tanaka-san reported to the ancestral shades on
his new status. Perhaps he related the changes which he had helped
to bring about in the village land-holding system, confident that the
news was acceptable to the invisible guest and that his new status gave
him an honorable place in the family annals.

Settling Land Payments

One could agree that the success of the land transfer phase of the operation seemed assured. Landlord resistance had failed to halt the land commissions. Tenant loyalties had finally swung to full support of the reform. Somehow, in spite of mechanical imperfections and government wrangling, the commissions had managed to learn their jobs and to work effectively. But the task of transferring the land, although in itself a major undertaking, was not the whole story of the reform. Several important aspects had been deliberately neglected in order to accomplish the land transfer itself on schedule. And as the transfer period passed its climax and drew near completion, these deferred phases loomed ever larger in scope and importance.

The first and most important of these auxiliary jobs was to secure payment for the land. This meant payment by the government to the landlords for the land purchased from them and collection of payment from the tenant by the government for the land which they had purchased. In the eyes of the Occupation, the matter of payment was crucial. The words "purchase and sale" connoted much of the distinction between a land reform in terms of private property institutions and the ownership of land by the state. To emphasize this aspect, the Occupation had laid down a hard and fast rule that payment, or contracts for payment, were to accompany all transfers. Payment, prompt payment to landlords, and by tenants, signified that the land was purchased, not seized, that it had been sold and not given away. Further, the importance of these final settlements was enhanced by the promptness with which they were made.

Because of the crucial nature of the payment aspect, Occupation officials naively assumed that the Japanese government was prepared to carry it out. But late in 1947 it became apparent that the Japanese had made no efforts to obtain final settlements and had made no real plans for handling the job. The accepted method by which the government ordinarily settled accounts with citizens to whom it owed money required a citizen to file a claim against the government. Then if the government chose, it might recognize the claim. The Japanese had thought that they would use a similar procedure in making final settlement with the landlords. By the time the Occupation had made this discovery, it was already too late to hope that the final settlement of accounts could be accomplished by the end of 1948. The Japanese declared flatly that if they attempted a full-scale financial settlement by that date, the land transfer program could not be accomplished.

These final settlements represented a tremendous volume of work. Moreover the task was enormously complicated by the dispersed character of the Japanese farm holdings. Altogether the government owed the landlords from whom land had been taken not less than twelve billion yen. At the same time, the government must collect in cash and payment contracts a comparable amount from the tenants who had received land. But separate payments and collections had to be

calculated for each separate parcel of land for which a writ of purchase or sale had been issued. Tenants, for example, had acquired
their new holdings in separate parcels and at different transfer dates.
Thus a single tenant, in acquiring an acre of land, might have purchased five or six different parcels. Each parcel might have been
acquired at a different time and quite probably had been owned originally by a different landlord. To complicate matters further, each
tenant was entitled to determine whether he wished to pay for his new
land in a lump sum or by means of a cash down payment plus a long-
term purchase contract.

Final settlement thus involved over twelve million separate transactions. Even by western standards of simplified routines and
mechanical aids, this procedure meant a lot of paper work. Under
more tedious Japanese methods the job was appalling.

This assignment was mainly a job for government forces in which
the land commissions could provide little assistance. But since the
burden of the work occurred at the village level, the commission
clerks were pressed into service. Unfortunately this increased burden of work was not accompanied by increased compensation. The
Diet, intent on balancing the budget, refused to consider a request for
additional clerical assistance, compensation, or incidental expenses.
As a result, commission clerks began to be thoroughly fed up. With
the transfer period drawing to a close they saw as their only reward
for faithful service an increased work load, an uncertain employment
future, and low pay. Many clerks requested assurance that their
services would be continued after the close of the reform. When this
assurance was not forthcoming, some quit their jobs; others simply
slowed down the rate at which they worked. While a great many
worked harder than ever, the defections and lowered morale made it
necessary to reschedule the date of completion of the transfer period,
moving it ahead to the end of March, 1949.

The work of making final settlements commenced in earnest in the
summer of 1948. Unexpected obstacles immediately appeared. The
bonds which the government had undertaken to deliver to the landlords
in payment for their lands were not available. The government en-
graving establishment simply could not prepare the bonds on schedule.
Settlement with absentee landlords was impeded because they could
not be located. Yet, as in the land transfer phase, an enormous over-
loading of the working staff and the imposition of incredibly long hours
finally resulted in progress. One doubts very much if western workers
faced with a similar situation would have been willing to undergo the
hardships that the Japanese workers accepted. It is questionable if
they could have stood up physically under the pressure.

The results were better than the Occupation had dared to hope.
By the end of March, 1949, over 64 per cent of all amounts due the
government by tenant purchasers had been collected and about half the
amount due to landlords by the government had been paid. By mid-
summer of that year, the assignment was almost completed and the
last details were finished early in 1950.

Registering Transferred Land

In a similar fashion the American specialists set out the firm requirement that evidence of valid title must be given to each new owner for each parcel of land acquired through the land reform program. GHQ specialists viewed the whole transfer operations, including payment for the land, as incomplete until Tanaka-san had a deed to his newly acquired property safely in his possession. They insisted that the official land registration books show a complete and accurate record of his ownership.

The Japanese bureaucracy did not altogether share this view. As in the case of payments, they preferred to wait until Tanaka-san asked them to make an official record of his ownership. But the Americans regarded such a procedure as exceedingly dangerous. They insisted that the whole process of the reform must culminate in a recorded transfer of title. They felt that this was an essential step which would make the whole land reform process irrevocable. They had no intention of permitting the reform to be upset in future years, after the Occupation had been withdrawn, by the discovery of legal discrepancies which might invalidate Tanaka-san's title. They wanted to be sure that the reform could not be reversed for any technical reason.

Among the tenants, too, there was a strong sentiment for completing the title registration. Canny, hard-headed little Tanaka-san was ignorant of the law, but he had a tremendous respect for the writings in the land register. As far as he was concerned, the final test of the validity of his new title was the land register. Only when his possession was recorded in that document would he finally be convinced that land reform was a reality. Despite official assurance of the validity of his new title, despite the public notice fluttering on the public bulletin board at the village office, despite written notices from the land commission and communications signed by the Minister of Agriculture, he remained skeptical. Only when all these facts had been reduced to an entry in the land register could he enjoy the full sense of possession.

Consummation of registration for all the lands involved in the reform program could not be achieved within the time limits set for completion of the reform. Again an enormous detailed job had to be faced. Full registration signified making sixty million separate entries for thirty million parcels of land scattered from one end of Japan to the other. It required a substantial increase in the staff not only of the Ministry of Agriculture but a large increase in the personnel of the Ministry of Justice as well. Again the Diet and the Ministry of Finance were unwilling to cooperate, refusing to provide the necessary funds. As a result, registration lagged in spite of the best efforts of those responsible for its completion. This work was not finally completed until the spring of 1951. Thus, although the actual transfer of land under the reform statutes was largely accomplished in the two-year period ending in 1948 as originally planned, the full legal transfer

was not completed for over four years from the commencement
of the operations.

By the end of 1948 a total of 4,529,538 acres of cultivated land had
been acquired from landlords. Of this amount tenants had received
4,255,530 acres. In the final wind-up, which ran for several months
longer, tenants received a total 4,829,175 acres. In addition, 864,247
acres of pasture land also passed into the hands of former tenants.

Failure In Compensating for Transferred Land

But, as the old saying goes, one can't make an omelet without
breaking eggs. Great achievements always have their costs. There
have been no bloodless wars and few great political achievements are
made save at some cost, however slight, to moral principle, dignity,
and honor. Even the best planned construction projects, where the
quantities involved are so relatively measurable and controllable
never are built precisely as planned. There must be improvisation
when unforeseen factors suddenly present themselves. So it was with
the Land Reform Program. For in spite of a great over-all success,
there were also costly mistakes which gave some blemish to the final
result although perhaps not seriously affecting its chief value to Japan
or its own general significance.

The principal shortcoming of the reform operations and the only
one for which a reasonably satisfactory adjustment could not be made
was the failure to pay the original landowners an adequate price for
their land. This failure was not the result of design or intent but of
the interplay of a number of factors. It falls under the head of government and economic malfunction. Despite vigorous efforts to find
a solution, there was no method of overcoming the joint effects of the
widespread monetary inflation interacting with the characteristic
rigidity of the Japanese government machinery.

The legal price for land, set originally by statute in 1938, was
later reaffirmed as a part of the general wartime price control structure. Unfortunately the inflation control measures did not effectively
offset the inflation. This effect rendered the official price for land
continually more unrealistic, while at the same time the administrative and legal framework prevented any upward adjustment in its
official price. In the end, landlords received too little for their land,
while tenants were the beneficiaries of an unplanned bonus. Of course
the landlord animus against the program was considerably inflamed
by the almost daily decline in the value of the money price of their
land. Tenant apprehension, too, was increased rather than alleviated
as they observed the working of the strange phenomena of inflation.

In October, 1946, when the Land Reform Law was enacted, the official price for land was about right. Yet by March, 1947, the effects
of inflation were beginning to make the official price appear unreason-
ably low in relation to other prices. Even so, if the government had
been able to buy and pay for all the land in a single transaction, the

harm might not have been too great. But this transaction was impossible. As we have seen, the capacity and structure of the Japanese government could not encompass such a task. As it was, the conduct of the program placed an enormous burden on government. A greater burden would have meant a distortion of the entire structure of government for the sake of a single agrarian program.

Of course all the land owned by landlords became subject to the law at the same time. But whether a particular piece of land was actually purchased at the beginning of the program or one year or two years later was largely a matter of chance. Nevertheless, the principle of equality before the law required that all the land so purchased receive the same price – same money price – actually, because of the inflation, a very different money value. Again this discrepancy might have worked to the advantage of some landowners had the government been able to make payment at the time the land was actually acquired. As it was, that possibility was offset by the government's inability to start financial settlements until nearly eighteen months after the commencement of the program. Yet if the government had devised a sliding scale so that later sellers received a larger price, it would have enormously complicated the settlement procedure and placed a premium on delay in enforcement of the program.

The government argued that its 1938 law and subsequent land price control measures had been deliberately designed to remove agricultural land from the class of commodities subject to speculation. In their eyes, investments in land had been placed by these measures in the same class as investments in fixed income bearing securities, life insurance, and savings accounts. Of course this entire class of investors were severely damaged by the inflation. Yet it could not be shown that investors in land suffered a greater hardship than other investors in this class. For this reason the Japanese government was reluctant to change its land price policy.

Although the Occupation endeavored to solve the problem of inequitable land prices, they were unable to do so. Each alternative proposal for solution proved unworkable. It was suggested, for example, that landlords should have been paid in terms of rice or other agricultural staples. The idea here was to give the landlord, as full purchase price for his land, the total of three or four years' harvest in the commodity or in its cash equivalent. But the prices of all agricultural commodities were very strictly controlled. Consumer needs were met by a strict rationing system. Rice and other staples were rigorously collected from the farmers. The amount of his produce which a farmer could retain for his own use was also regulated. Finally the price which the farmer received was controlled. Consequently, any settlement with landlords in terms of commodities would have required a complex adjustment within the price-rationing system. Landlords could not have been given staple crops to do with as they pleased. Such a procedure would have immediately aggravated the serious black market situation.

Yet if the money equivalent of rice had been given the landlords, the price would have had to be in line with official fixed prices and the original problem of land price would thus merely have been stated in different terms. Any fixed price would shortly have been out of adjustment with new levels of inflated prices. Finally, if different commodity prices were set for land settlement purposes with lower prices at the beginning of the period and higher prices in the latter portion, then the same incentives for deferment of enforcement would have appeared as in the cases of different prices for the land itself.

At any rate no solution was found. In the end, all landlords received the same legal rate for their land regardless of the actual purchase date. The failure to find a flexible land-pricing formula plus the delayed payments resulted in a serious loss to these owners. While this loss may be explained, it can hardly be justified. The factors which brought it about are clear, but the solution still remains a puzzle. Future designers of land reform programs should surely recognize this problem and attempt to solve it at the outset.

It is unfortunate that up to the present time the case for agrarian reform, in the regions where it is needed, becomes self-evident only in times of great crisis when the entire economy, rural and industrial, is convulsed and partially destroyed. Those of us who went through the Japanese experience certainly could wish that future agrarian reforms be executed in periods uncomplicated by the kind of postwar displacement and devastation so hampering to the Japanese program. The sweeping changes which a thorough land reform entails can be put into effect in the midst of disturbed general conditions only at the expense of extraordinary burdens on those charged with responsibility for the program. Such burdens may be carried heroically, but not always without error.

Other Shortcomings of the Reform

In spite of the shortcomings which have been described, the reform itself succeeded. In view of the handicaps, the achievement may even be termed spectacular. Yet the reform was not a panacea. Serious deficiencies in the Japanese land holding system remain. Probably the most important of these is the long-run trend toward ever smaller farm holdings. Along with this trend is a tendency to increase the number of tiny plots which comprise the individual holding.

These two factors have their origin in the conflict between the terribly limited land resources of Japan and the ever increasing population. In spite of the benefits of land reform this situation spells a dark future for Tanaka-san and more particularly for his sons and grandsons. If the size of their holding is allowed to decrease, they will become poorer and poorer. Perhaps we have been able to convey the impression that the Japanese farmer is already very poor and works very hard. Fully to comprehend this point, we should understand that the so-called law of diminishing returns does not exist for many Japanese farmers. They do not calculate their efforts on the basis of a margin where inputs of labor equal increased value of product. The only margin for the Orient is the border between existence and starvation. Even though Tanaka-san's return decreases for each hour he works, he still must toil on. The poorer he is, the smaller is his holding. And so he must work all the harder. He must continue to toil so long as there is any return at all for his labor. He is not concerned that in these circumstances his labor finally becomes very, very cheap. And the real meaning of his poverty is that as a producer he becomes worth less and less. Thus he farms ten or a dozen tiny plots, moving ceaselessly between them, a large fraction of his working time spent in walking between the various portions of his farm.

But in addition to wasting time and energy, the scattered and dispersed nature of the individual farms also wastes land, the most precious resource of all. The maze of pathways, property lines, drainage ways, and irrigated ditches conform to the crazy quilt pattern of holdings (see accompanying illustration). Indeed, it has been calculated that a rationalization of this pattern through a consolidation of holdings would make available an additional 10 or 15 per cent of the present arable land of Japan. It would also save as much as 20 per cent of the labor now required to farm the present area.

Unless these negative forces are counteracted, the ensuing poverty may produce the conditions from which tenancy or a condition closely akin to it will result. There are two ways in which this problem can be attacked: by controlling the scope of land inheritance and by rationalizing the dispersed character of the farm holdings. At the outset planners of the land reform program, recognizing the significance of land dispersion, sought to incorporate a land consolidation program within the framework of the reform legislation. They visualized a process by which the land transfer would have been accompanied by an extensive trading of individual tracts so that the final result would have been unified holdings for the new owners. Unfortunately they failed to accomplish the consolidation objective because neither tenants nor landowners were willing to part with the lands traditionally cultivated by their families.

It mattered little whether Tanaka-san was landowner or tenant, he resisted equally any efforts to separate him from the lands which, whether by ownership or agreement, he was accustomed to cultivate. In spite of the excessive waste of his labor and the self-evident inefficiency, he clung to the ancestral lands. Moreover, neither Japanese law nor the powers of the Occupation conferred any right to disturb landowners who were not landlords. Such owners could not be coerced to dispose of their lands through sale or by trading it for the lands of others unless their holdings exceeded the legal limit of 7.5 acres. Since this limit had been set as a maximum based on actual statistical calculation of Japanese farm size, there were only a small number of owner-cultivators whose holdings were excessive. But lands cultivated

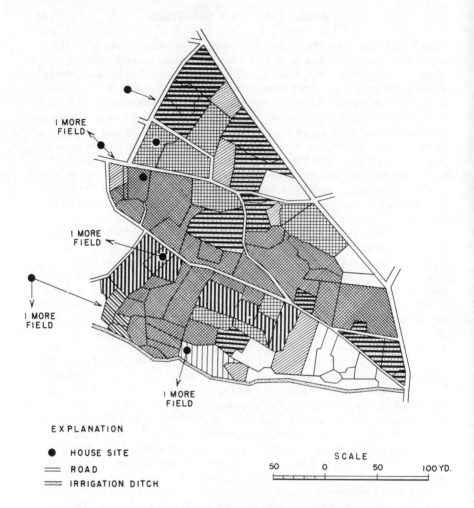

EXPLANATION

● HOUSE SITE
═══ ROAD
〰〰 IRRIGATION DITCH

SCALE

50   0   50   100 YD.

FROM GENERAL HEADQUARTERS, SUPREME COMMANDER FOR THE ALLIED POWERS
NATURAL RESOURCES SECTION REPORT NO. 136 – BY PERMISSION

Number and location of 70 plots operated by seven farmers in Suye Mura,
Kumamoto prefecture. (Taken from *The Japanese Village in Transition,*
Natural Resources Section Report No. 136.)

by tenants were dispersed and intermingled among the equally dispersed holdings of legitimate owner-cultivators in a completely haphazard fashion. Thus a consolidation of farm units necessarily involved all farm lands. While tenants might have been forced to accept consolidation by law, without voluntary cooperation from owner-cultivators there could be no effective consolidation. Such cooperation was not forthcoming and the program failed. There were a few exceptions to this general failure. In these instances, land consolidation or "land amelioration" came about through exceptionally able village leadership. Yokogoshi village in Niigata prefecture has developed such a program. As a result, farm yields have increased ten per cent. Even so, the farmers still complain about the elimination of their ancient fields.

The second problem, that of halting a decline in the size of farms by restricting the impact of inheritance rights on farm lands is more difficult to solve than land consolidation. Yet it is clear that the rate of diminution of holdings proceeds more rapidly in countries with limited land resources whose customs and laws sanction the equal division of the patrimony among all the heirs. In other countries the disastrous final result was so plain for both the farm population and the general welfare that the rights to the inheritance of land were strictly curbed. Among the Japanese this curbing of inheritance rights came about quite naturally through the family arrangement known as the *house system*. Under this arrangement, every Japanese was part of a firm-knit family group or *house*. House headship, including the inheritance of property, passed normally from father to eldest son.

The Japanese house system was fundamental to the entire structure of Japanese society. The supremacy of the house over the individual was the starting point of a whole series of controls exercised by the *buraku*, the village, and the Empire over the lives and fortunes of the Japanese people. Each member of a house derived his basic status from his position in the house and this came about largely as an accident of birth. Each member thus attained a certain position at birth and, except in the case of the eldest son, this position was unchanged throughout his or her entire life. A younger brother remained a junior member of the house and women members, although occasionally occupying positions of honor, usually exercised little authority even over their own fortunes or acts. The system was almost entirely authoritarian and anti-democratic. Its existence was an essential feature of those aspects of the institutional life of Japan singled out for reform by the Allied Occupation. The house system itself was marked for abolition. Now, existence of the house system depended to a considerable degree on laws governing inheritance of property specified both in the Japanese constitution and the civil code. Legal abolition of the house system along with many other undemocratic and repressive legal institutions was accomplished through establishment of the new Japanese constitution of May, 1947, and by a complete

revision of the former civil code. With installation of these new instruments the ancient Japanese house system ceased to exist.

Under the new laws all members of a Japanese family were entitled
to share equally in the property of the parent. In the case of farm
families, family holdings which had remained intact for generations
were now subject to partition among all the surviving heirs. Thus one
important political reform was gained at the cost of possible ruin of
the Japanese peasantry. In their zeal to accomplish the political reform, the American political advisers failed to consider that the land
inheritance system as it had developed in the rural village had provided an answer to the special needs of Japanese farming and Japanese
farmers.

It is regrettable that some compromise could not have been reached
between the very real need to abolish the house system and the very
great danger to which the Japanese rural economy is exposed as a
result of the working of the principle of unlimited succession. Efforts
of the agricultural specialists in GHQ to exempt agricultural lands
from the unlimited succession principle were unavailing. General
MacArthur's political and legal advisers were firmly opposed to any
modification of the constitution or the new civil code. In fact they regarded these particular reforms as embodying the essence of the Occupation mission. Unfortunately they were unfamiliar with the practical considerations of farming and farm life. As men of principle
they insisted on complete democratization of Japan in a somewhat
legalistic meaning of the term. They seemed to have the faith common to some men of the law that by doing what they considered to be
legal, justice and right would prevail though the heavens fell. They
might be criticized for a certain lack of flexibility and common sense
but never for a failure to meet a moral challenge. They "seen their
duty and they done it!"

Yet the evidence in various heavily populated parts of the world is
overwhelmingly against unlimited inheritance. Agricultural economists are all too familiar with the woeful results which this principle
can bring about. In the United States, one of the agricultural problem areas of the country is Taos county, New Mexico. Here the
principle of unlimited succession rights among Spanish American
farmers had produced results which could never be more than partially corrected. In some of the valleys of Utah the progressive decrease in the size of holdings with each new generation threatens the
economic stability of several communities. In both China and India
this principle has brought near disaster in certain regions. Indian
scholars have blamed the introduction by the British of the western
principle of unlimited succession for the continuous decline of farm
size in the Deccan.

With these facts in mind the agricultural specialists of GHQ continued to protest the new inheritance system. Drafts of legislation to
protect Japanese agricultural lands against the inevitable mathematics
of reproduction were prepared by the Japanese agricultural officials

in collaboration with Occupation agricultural specialists in 1947, 1948, and 1949. In the case of the 1947 and 1948 drafts, approval was withheld by General MacArthur's legal and political advisers. As a result the measures never reached the Diet. A 1949 draft was so badly cut up in an effort to meet the objection of the legal and political technicians that the Diet was unable to understand it and refused to consider it. A similar measure was under study by the Diet in 1950 and again in 1951.

Efforts to provide legal framework to facilitate a land consolidation program met a better fate. As a result of the unsatisfactory outcome of the attempt to combine land consolidation with land reform the two programs were separated. After careful study it was decided to approach land consolidation not as a narrow problem of individual farms, but as an aspect of land as a vital natural resource. Thus the consolidation of scattered holdings into a compact block was fitted into a broader program of land conservation and development. Around this principle a long-term program of education and planning could be developed. Tanaka-san could not be forced to consolidate his holdings, but he might be persuaded to accept the principle if he could come to appreciate all the other gains which were entailed in a broad land improvement program.

Work on drafting such broad land improvement legislation began early in 1948. The new legislation was introduced in the Diet in May, 1949, and enacted as the Land Improvement Law on June 6, 1949. The measure provides Japan with a model land improvement law which makes it easy for local communities to form land improvement districts. Necessary technical help is provided to plan and execute the development that is best fitted to local needs.

Activity under the new law commenced in 1950. The first step was the drafting, with the help and consent of rural communities, of a five-year land consolidation program comprising four million acres. Over a thousand separate consolidation projects involving over one million acres were scheduled for completion by the end of 1951.

In the outcome of these subsidiary aspects of the land reform program discussed here the Occupation must accept at least partial responsibility for success and failure. In forcing a timely and definitive execution of final settlements and title registration, the whole land reform program was successfully rescued from uncertainty and a clouded future. The land was bought and paid for. New owners received indisputable proof of possession. Legally, the reform was nailed down tight. Unfortunately, the combination of a serious postwar inflation and the rigidity of government functioning resulted in a land-pricing arrangement which left much to be desired. Here, the Occupation was unable to find an answer to the dilemma. Perhaps there was no answer; nevertheless, the resulting situation must be recognized as a defect in the operation of the reform. Again, preoccupation with the legal side of democratic reforms has resulted in exposing Japanese agriculture to the serious dangers of unlimited subdivision

through inheritance. This situation can cause only the greatest concern to those who have studied with care the problems of Japanese
agrarian life. One can only hope that the Japanese themselves will
find an answer to this terrible problem without sacrificing essential
features of the new democratic framework. On the other hand, the
Occupation must be credited with helping to develop a first-class land
improvement law. Through this law it is now possible to attack the
problem of consolidating into efficient units the woefully scattered and
dispersed holdings that make up the Japanese farms. In the long run,
provided the inheritance problem is overcome, the impact of this
principle may have an even greater effect on the Japanese farmer than
the reform itself. This is true because the establishment of a ration-
ally planned farm unit permits the introduction of self-conscious
planning of agricultural operations, the introduction of mechanical
labor-saving devices, and the revaluation of farm labor.

Chapter 14

SAYONARA

ONCE again we take the long downhill road to Oharame. Still the ancient road curves beside the terraced fields. Crossing and recrossing the rushing mountain torrent, it passes the cluster of houses that make up the several *buraku* of Oharame. If we halt our downward journey and listen, we hear again the hum of the Japanese countryside. It is the same everywhere, at Oharame, at Nisi Susa, at Higashi Sawada, or at little Nadabun on the plains of Shimane. The rhythm of rural life is unbroken. Ceaselessly the cycle of work goes on. Endlessly, the demands of the fields are met by the never ending toil of the Japanese farm people.

But now our task with these fields and these people is done. It is late in 1951 and the Allied Occupation has run its course. Historians of the future will probably debate the Occupation's merits and consider whether it should have lasted for a longer or a shorter period. But the facts are that now it is almost time for a somewhat reorganized and rehabilitated Japan to seek a new destiny, free of the restrictions which have been imposed upon it during the past six years — years which have witnessed the expenditure of much effort to bring to Oharame, to Nisi Susa, to Nadabun, and to the thousands of other villages of the mountains and plains a better way of life.

It has been the hope and the plan that rural Japan, representing some 40 per cent of the total Japanese population, can become a strong, self-determining segment of the national society. If this objective is accomplished, not only will Japan become a great nation again, but the citizenry can move forward together in united purpose as free people.

Transition to Owner Operation

When the Occupation commenced, more than four million Japanese families, over 60 per cent of the total farm population, lived out their daily lives to a greater or less degree under the thralldom of an antiquated and feudal tenancy system. The area farmed by these folk amounted to 46 per cent of all the cultivated lands of Japan. Tenants paid rents equal to not less than half the produce from their tiny plots. Not only was the Japanese rural village a repository of feudalism but it was almost a national symbol of ancient and outmoded customs. In

141

a sense, rural Japan remained as a captive economy. It was deliberately maintained in a backward and semidependent condition so that it might the more easily be fitted into the plans of the Empire builders.

But by 1951, over three and a half million tenant families had been helped to a position of ownership of much of the land they cultivated. Whereas formerly well over seven million acres were owned by landlords, today less than 1.5 million acres are rented (see accompanying illustration). And these lands are leased under the strictest supervision of democratically elected land commissions. Fair play between landlords and tenants is now fully guaranteed. Tenancy, an economic and social institution largely tinctured with feudal carryovers, has been completely abolished. A small remaining area of rented land is operated under the terms of modern contract negotiations. Today there are perhaps less than 500,000 farmers in Japan who rent all the land they cultivate and most of these are found in fishing villages where farming is only a part-time vocation. Aside from this group, there is no farmer in all Japan who does not own at least some of the land he cultivates.

Yet in spite of speed, the program was always orderly. Never was agricultural production significantly impeded. On the contrary, the harvests of Japan increased considerably in the six years of Allied Occupation. While the program was marked by a vigorous opposition by some landlords, these disputes did not approach widespread disorder. At times, life in the villages was strained and personal relations were ruffled. But the basic solidarity of the Japanese rural village as a social institution was not threatened. There was no displacement nor dislocation either of people or of rural life in general.

Operations always proceeded within the confines of the law and of judicial process. In a little more than three years (1947, 1948, 1949) a far-reaching social and economic change of the greatest importance, not alone for the people of the Japanese islands but for all the farmers of Asia as well, was brought about. Doubtless, critics of the accomplishment are to be found. But in spite of all these, the fact that several million people, formerly without the slightest stake in private property, have been enabled to obtain possession of the land they cultivate and to obtain some voice in the design and pattern of their own destiny, cannot be obscured.

The Japanese villages have undergone a thoroughly disturbing experience. Many old social inequities based on land ownership have completely disappeared. Landlordism has disappeared, but the individual landlords still remain in the village and still retain their dignity. Likewise the tenant class, as formerly constituted, has completely disappeared. The individuals who comprised the tenant group have attained a new stature possessing the dignity of free men. Thus the two former classes are replaced by a greatly enlarged body of owner-cultivators, now the most significant social influence in the village.

Along with the changes in the ownership of land has gone a considerable shift in the important sociological factors of leadership and

EFFECT OF LAND REFORM

CHANGES IN DEGREE OF OWNER OPERATION

BEFORE SEPT. 2, 1945
FARMLAND WAS

SINCE JAN. 1, 1949
FARMLAND IS

OWNER OPERATED
54%

TENANT OPERATED
46%

OWNER OPERATED
88%

TENANT
OPERATED
12%

CHANGES IN TENURE STATUS

BEFORE SEPT. 2, 1945

SINCE JAN. 1, 1949

TENANTS
26.7%

OWNERS
36.5%

PART TENANT
PART OWNER
36.8%

OWNERS
70%

TENANTS
5.5%

PART TENANT
PART OWNER
24.5%

FROM GENERAL HEADQUARTERS, SUPREME COMMANDER FOR THE ALLIED POWERS
NATURAL RESOURCES SECTION REPORT NO. 127 – BY PERMISSION

Land reform—changes in degree of owner operation. (Taken from *Japanese Land Reform*—Natural Resources Section Report No. 127.)

status. At the outset of the program, tenants were more or less
forced to assume leadership on the land commissions. With this
status as a start, a number of tenants have gone on to even more
responsible positions as mayors and village assemblymen. In 1948,
Arthur Raper of the United States Department of Agriculture discovered that more than two-thirds of all the public officials in the thirteen villages which he studied were holding office for the first time.
Many of these, under the old system, would never have dared to
cherish such ambitions. Indeed, the experiences of the tenant members of the land commissions were a training in public affairs which
prepared many of them for the leadership role they now play in village affairs. So land reform, in addition to its specific function, has
been unexcelled as an instrument for adult education.

Yet all these gains have been achieved without serious humiliation
or loss of face to the landlords. Some of them, perhaps, bitterly opposed the reform, but the program was designed to avoid personal
clashes. Landlords have been somewhat reduced in social status.
Nevertheless, as we see it now, the over-all effect has been to raise
the social status of tenants a great deal and to reduce landlord status
moderately.

Most landlords still hold the respect of their village associates.
Some still occupy positions of leadership. However, this leadership
now rests on a solid basis of personal merit, rather than on the prerogatives of inherited position. A number of landlords have engaged
in business ventures within the village. Some have become sawmill
operators. Others have entered the merchandising field. Still others
are now in the service trades. One landlord, of Yokogoshi in Niigata
prefecture, turned his home into a museum, arranging to have the
house designated as a branch of the National Museum. Another former
landlord, of Kumano village in Hiroshima prefecture, formerly owned
122.5 acres of tenanted land. He now cultivates 2.7 acres himself and
leases out one acre. The balance was all transferred to tenants.
Formerly, a member of the Diet, this individual now proposes to run
for the Diet again. He will probably be elected since his neighbors
still have a genuine respect for him. His leadership position seems
to have suffered very little, but his worldly estate apparently has
declined somewhat, for although he still lives in a fine house, he no
longer keeps any servants.

In Yamaguchi town in Yamaguchi prefecture another landlord who
owned 171 acres of tenanted land, which has been purchased from him,
has started a girls' finishing school. He still owns considerable forest
land and has substantial cash assets. Still another former landlord,
Mr. Tanabe of Yoshida village in Shimane prefecture, formerly owned
nearly two thousand acres of cultivated land. He now retains only 1.7
acres of this kind of land. Of his original holding of over 35,000 acres
of forest land, he still retains 22,000 acres. One of the landlords who
took a most cooperative attitude toward the reform program, Mr.
Tanabe is highly respected in the village. Perhaps as a result of land

reform, he has become very active in business. He now heads a local sawmilling concern and is also the head of a thriving charcoal enterprise.

While such incidents of the transition of landlords are not altogether representative of all the changes affecting landlords, they do perhaps give a clue to the kind of adjustment which many landlords are making. Tenants for their part have settled into their new positions rather quietly and also with dignity. There has been no crowing or exultation. Yet, in spite of their inconspicuous behavior, the new landowners have let it be known, in no uncertain fashion, that they prefer their new status to the old and intend to retain it at all costs.

But as Dr. MacMahon Ball has pointed out, "It would be foolish to hope for too much from these reform measures, even if they are carried out according to plan. By enabling a tenant to become an owner-farmer you improve his condition by increasing his rights, particularly his rights to a larger share of what he produces. But you do not necessarily increase the volume or value of his products. It is often said that farming is very efficient in Japan. This is true in the sense that the Japanese are expert in getting the maximum product from a given area. But the meticulous exploitation of every cultivable square yard is carried on only by the reckless expenditure of human labor."[1]

It is quite true that if we look only at the material gain which Japanese farmers have made through the land reform program, the benefits do not appear overly impressive. That evaluation is partly because we Westerners are accustomed to statistics both of production and distribution which are quite impressively astronomical. Perhaps too, many of us in the Western world are completely unfamiliar with the quantitative side of Asiatic poverty. In that region, any increase at all in consumption may make the difference between outright starvation and tolerable malnutrition.

For a quantitative picture of the effect of land reform on farm income, let us consider the effect on rice farming as representative, since rice lands constituted about half of all the lands which were transferred. The total acreage of rice land transferred to tenants amounted to 2.7 million acres which have an average yield of about 40 bushels per acre. The average rice rental was rarely less than half the crop; frequently it was much higher. Thus we may assume that the landlord formerly took about 20 bushels per acre for his rent. If we interpret the land reform program in terms of what it means to the income of those rice farmers who were formerly tenants, we may say that their annual economic gain is measured perhaps by 50 million bushels of rice which formerly as tenants they paid as rent and which as owner-farmers they now retain. In the case of the individual farmer of the average sized 2.5 acre holding, his gross crop would have been in the neighborhood of 100 bushels. Today he keeps the

---

[1]This quotation from Dr. MacMahon Ball's *Japan – Enemy or Ally* (Melbourne: Cassell and Co. Ltd., 1948), pp. 143, 144, was used in *Japanese Land Reform*, p. 94.

whole product whereas formerly he gave his landlord 50 bushels and
kept 50 for himself. At the same time, we must remember that well
over one million Japanese farmers cultivate less than 1.5 acres. On
a farm this size the rice crop would be 60 bushels and the rent would
have been 30 bushels. On farms of this size the change is even more
significant, since a 30-bushel standard of living is slim indeed.

What of Future Needs?

While Japanese farmers, as a group, have received limited economic relief through the land reform program, they are by no means
well off. By any Western standards they are very poor indeed. Not-
withstanding the gains afforded by land reform, agrarian Japan still
presents a picture of great economic and social need. Moreover,
some of these needs are so pressing that some means of meeting
them must be discovered if the land reform gains are to be preserved.
Japan is a part of Asia and Asia from end to end is a great rural poor-
house. Temporarily, Japanese farmers are above the average level
of Asiatic misery, but if they are to avoid the general fate of Asian
farmers, it is obvious that the progress represented by the land reform program must be reinforced by a number of important adjustments.

Every tendency in Japanese political thought which accepts the
traditional view that rural living conditions may be allowed to lag
behind other segments of the economy must be regarded as hostile to
progress and democracy in Japan. There can be no concessions to
commerce or industry at the expense of lowered rural living standards. Indeed positive steps must be taken to protect Japanese agricultural producers from commercial and metropolitan exploitation.
One means by which Japanese husbandmen can receive partial insurance of both maximum production and maximum income is through
the great system of farmer-owned cooperatives fostered by the Occupation and established by the Ministry of Agriculture and Forestry.
This system needs constant support and improvement to insure that
farmers achieve bargaining equality with the remainder of the nation.
Such bargaining equality is an essential prerequisite to rural economic health.

Equally great is the need of Japanese farmers for credit at moderate interest rates. This need has not been met; indeed the principal
source of rural credit has been a disgraceful system of private usury
which has seriously handicapped agrarian development. In the past,
usury and landlordism went hand in hand to create the nightmare of
tenancy. It is alarming that even at the present time the Japanese
banking interests, both public and private, have failed to display real
interest in providing for rural credit needs. Yet, there can be no
doubt that, unless a modern agricultural credit system is established,
there can be no lasting stability in Japanese agriculture.

Japanese farmers, along with the rest of the nation, face a long period of heavy taxation. Agriculture must bear its fair share of this burden. However, unfair rural tax policies contributed greatly to the benighted conditions of the rural areas as they existed at the end of the war. In addition to its distinct lack of justice, the former rural tax system was grossly unscientific. Tax collectors made levies against the instruments of production and thus reduced the productive capacity of cultivators. Still worse, little attention was given to the matter of adjusting taxes in accordance with ability to pay, or to earning capacity. Moreover, local levies were haphazard and uncertain. Indeed, there seemed to be little awareness, among those who made the fiscal policy of the nation, of the distinctive character of agricultural production, when it came to assessing or collecting rural taxes. Even today, it is doubtful whether the Ministry of Finance concerns itself overmuch with developing a sound public finance policy for agriculture. This is discouraging because careless or antiquated tax policies will greatly diminish the benefits of land reform and may result in a loss of agricultural production.

Not quite so apparent, but even more fundamental, is the need for an enlightened, long-range program of general education for the adults and children of rural villages. While specific impediments such as poor soil and overpopulation have retarded progress, it is the backward and unenlightened simplicity of many farmers that has probably been their greatest handicap. To a very considerable extent, lack of education and even of ordinary information has tended to make rural folk the dupes of more sophisticated political and economic elements. A great deal of thought and care has gone into recent efforts to improve rural education. But the advance is still very new. Sustained effort must be maintained for a long time if a really enlightened rural population is to emerge.

Japanese farmers also have great need for technical guidance to solve the many problems of agricultural production. These problems run the gamut from land management and fertilizer requirements to seed improvement and pest control. Stimulus from Occupation scientists and educators has resulted in the development of sound basic legislation to promote agricultural research and to make this research available to working farmers through a recently reorganized and modernized farm advisor system. This system must be expanded and improved.

But the day of the Occupation is over. The last Occupation official has departed from Nippon's shores. All the groundwork which was laid for the rehabilitation and liberation of rural Japan has passed into full control of the Japanese people and their leaders. This is as it should be. Nevertheless much of the future of agrarian Japan will depend on the intent and will of the new Japanese leaders and administrators. To them remains the task of consolidating and reaffirming the gains so recently made by the peasantry. The issue seems quite clear. If Japan is to become a strong democratic nation, then its rural folk must be placed permanently in a position to realize the values which only just now have been placed within their reach.

Most important of all is the urgent need for the rural people to become truly free. For centuries, as instruments of Imperial policy, they have been told what to do. Even the recent land reform and the other recent agrarian measures were enacted, not by rural leaders, but by government officials acting in behalf of farmers and without any political mandate from them. This is paternalism. As such, it must be replaced by self-determination. It is necessary, if democracy is to gain a foothold in Japan, that farm people develop a definite political consciousness and the ability to select their own leaders and spokesmen. The day of self-appointed spokesmen for rural interests must end.

Before this objective can be realized, Japan must have an enlightened and politically capable farm movement. It would be extremely dangerous to permit the continued existence of a large, potentially powerful, but unorganized and frustrated rural mass. Already we have seen the political capital which Japan's war lords made of this situation. It is altogether too easy a matter for astute politicians to exploit rural ignorance and backwardness for cynical and ruthless purposes. In today's unstable world any unenlightened group anywhere is a likely target for Communist exploitation. For this specific reason, if not for more altruistic motives, the political health of rural Japan and, for that matter, of all rural Asia, must be a matter of vital concern to the free world. Conversely, this political health cannot emanate from a bankrupt economic system.

But the responsibility for bringing about the conditions of political and economic health in rural Japan does not rest entirely with the Japanese. Japan will need friendship and understanding from the Western world if she is to become strong. It would be tragic indeed should the American people let the termination of the Allied Occupation signify the end of their interest in Japan. If this should happen, much of the pain and sacrifice that went into the Pacific war would be lost and along with it perhaps all the potentialities for good inherent in the work of the Occupation itself. At the present time, an alarmingly small number of Americans appreciate the great significance to the Japanese people and to all rural Asia of the Occupation's accomplishments in rural Japan.

Few Americans realize that to all intents and purposes, rural Asia *is* Asia. So both at home and abroad, we should make every effort to identify American democratic objectives with this Japanese achievement and with other similar achievements. We should expressly and forthrightly indicate our accord with the need for similar adjustments throughout Asia. Our participation in Japan's recent agrarian reforms should be a matter of pride. It represents America at her best. We have demonstrated in Japan the harmony of democratic beliefs and economic justice for agrarian people. We should capitalize perhaps more broadly on this performance and in louder tones. It is highly necessary — indeed, at the moment it is crucial — that Asiatic people learn that Americans recognize the reality of their distress and the reasonableness of their aspirations. These struggling peasants need to know that we are positively sympathetic to their suffering; that in particular, we earnestly desire to see their aspirations for a secure land tenure realized. It is clearly apparent that a great opportunity exists at this very moment for letting the people of Asia know that the American spirit of fair play, of equality, and of freedom is a great dynamic force in the world and that *it is on their side.*

*   *   *

But now the time for leave-taking is at hand. We have just been dealing with lofty matters of high policy, yet we must not forget the common courtesies of departure which polite people always observe. And among the Japanese, politeness is a charming virtue. Then, too, one always likes to take a last cup of tea with an old friend before a long journey. So we go to pay a final visit. To whom, you ask? Why, to our old friend Tanaka-san, of course!

As we leave the train at the little village station, he is waiting for us. And with him is Mrs. Tanaka in her very best kimono and obi. Bowing repeatedly and smiling profusely she greets us with all sorts of gracious good wishes. But that isn't all, for the whole family has turned out. There is elder brother, Masao, and younger brother, Minoru, who also bow and then a little awkwardly shake hands. Shyly in the background are the girls. Elder sister Takako too is in her best kimono, and finally there is our favorite, doll-like little eight-year-old sister Miyako, who wears her best blue serge school uniform skirt, white middy blouse, black stockings, and, joy of joys, Western style low-heeled patent leather slippers.

A happy group, we walk together up the village street, turning finally into the narrow winding way that leads to the Tanaka home. Each youngster has painstakingly learned a special English sentence for the occasion. Masao formally regrets our leaving and wishes for our early return. Minoru hopes we have learned to like Japan. Elder sister expresses a kind sentiment for our wife and family, and Miyako softly requests that some day we will write her a letter for she would like to write us a letter in English. We are all very glad to be together again, but a little sad too, for it is for the last time. Finally we enter the house, pausing to remove our shoes. Then we sit over the teacups, we of course in the place of honor before the alcove of the Tokonoma. Mrs. Tanaka and the girls busy themselves making us comfortable, seeing that our cup is full and passing the soybean cakes. It is very pleasant. And very reassuring too, for there is an atmosphere of strength and solidity about this family that reflects endurance and stability.

We talk, Tanaka-san and I. We speak of land reform and of his experiences as a land commissioner. He tells, with a chuckle, of some of the amusing incidents in the early hectic sessions of the commission.

We discuss village affairs and the changes that have been made and of others that are likely to occur. Then, with her housekeeping duties complete, Mrs. Tanaka joins us. She sits, not beside, but just a little back from us with the girls beside her. Then the talk gets around to their own affairs. Mrs. Tanaka bashfully alludes to the fact that in this fall's elections her husband was elected to the Village Assembly. We are pleased to hear of his recognition and congratulate Tanaka-san accordingly.

Finally the opportune time comes to ask a question. "How does it feel, Tanaka-san, to be a landowner after so many years as a tenant?" With this question, the whole family lights up. Each countenance is radiant with a quiet joy. Typical Japanese composure restrains the vivid emotion which nevertheless expresses itself in a sort of suffused glow. Tanaka-san tells us that it is now two years since he became a landowner, but that it is still hard to realize. He speaks of all the years when he yearned to buy a little land but realized always that his yearnings could never be more than fruitless dreams. His father and his grandfather before him had entertained similar hopeless yearnings. He says frankly that he, like all other Japanese tenant farmers, wanted to become a landowner more than anything else in the world. Land ownership was the unattainable pinnacle of his ambition. Now this wish is fulfilled and never, never will he allow himself to become a tenant again. He looks briefly at the eldest son and, although unspoken, we grasp the fleeting thought, "and when I go to my ancestors there will be land for my son."

It grows late. The visit to the Tanakas and to Japan is almost at an end. So we ask Tanaka-san to show us over the little "farm" which he has acquired through the land reform program. We all go out, putting on our shoes at the threshold. As we walk, younger brother, Minoru, stays close beside us on the left and little younger sister, Miyako, so grave and shy, slips her hand into ours on the right side. Tanaka-san walks ahead to show the way and the rest bring up the rear. We pass along rural pathways and over little bridges in a happy communion of friendship and a mutual sense of achievement. Then Tanaka-san points out the various plots that make up his holding. The soil is now quite dry and the paddy lands, empty of their harvests, are covered with a short stubble that gleams like silver in the late afternoon sunshine.

As we look at the fields, all the trials and painful exertions are submerged in a sense of triumph and an expanding sense of hope for the future of the Tanaka family and the millions of farm people it typifies. We turn to go—but a thought strikes us: "Let us go alone." And they, all the Tanakas, will remain, so that we may remember them always, standing together on their land. So it is, and at the little bridge before the main village street, we turn and look back.

There they all stand at last, father, mother, children—a little Japanese family with their feet firmly planted on the soil of Japan—that soil which means so much to them and to the future of their country. We wave a final farewell—sayonara, Good-bye, Tanaka-san. Good-bye, Japan. Good-bye! Good-bye!

BIBLIOGRAPHY

Books and Periodical Articles

Anezaki, Masaharu. *Art, Life, and Nature in Japan,* Boston: Marshall Jones and Company, 1932.

Asakawa, K., *The Documents of Iriki,* New Haven: Yale University Press, 1939.

Borton, Hugh, "Peasant Uprisings in Japan of the Tokugawa Period," *The Transactions of the Asiatic Society of Japan,* Second Series, Vol. XVI.

Ball, W. MacMahon, *Japan, Enemy or Ally?,* Melbourne: Cassell and Co., Ltd., 1948.

——————, "Reflections on Japan," *Pacific Affairs,* Vol. XXI, No. 1, March, 1948.

Byas, Hugh, *Government by Assassination,* New York: Alfred A. Knopf, 1942.

DeGaris, Frederic, *We Japanese* (2 vols.), Tokyo, 1946.

Embree, John F., *The Japanese Nation. A Social Survey,* New York: Farrar and Rhinehart, 1945.

——————, *Suye Mura, A Japanese Village,* Chicago: University of Chicago Press, 1944.

Hearn, Lafcadio, *Essays in European and Oriental Literature,* New York: Dodd, Mead and Co., 1923.

——————, *Exotics and Retrospectives,* Boston: Little, Brown and Co., 1898.

——————, *Japan,* New York: Grossett and Dunlap, 1904.

Hewes, Laurence I., Jr., *Japanese Land Reform Program,* Tokyo: General Headquarters, Supreme Commander for the Allied Powers, Natural Resources Section, Report No. 127, 1950.

——————, "Readjustment in Land Tenure in Japan," *Land Economics,* Vol. XXV, No. 3, August, 1949.

——————, *The Japanese Land Reform Program – Its Significance to Rural Asia,* Proceedings Thirteenth Annual National Farm Institute Feb. 16, 17, 1951, Des Moines, Iowa.

Honjo, E., "The Economic Thought in the Middle Period of the Tokugawa Era," *Kyoto University Economic Review,* Vol. XV, No. 4, October, 1940.

——————, "Changes of Social Classes During the Tokugawa Period," *Kyoto University Economic Review,* Vol. II, No. 2, December, 1927.

——————, "The Decay of the Samurai Class," *Kyoto University Economic Review,* Vol. II, No. 1, July, 1927.

——————, "The Agrarian Problem in the Tokugawa Regime," *Kyoto University Economic Review,* Vol. I, No. 2, December, 1926.

Horie, Y., "An Outline of Economic Policy in the Tokugawa Period," *Kyoto University Economic Review,* Vol. XV, No. 4, October, 1940.

Isobe, Hidetoshi, *Labour Conditions in Japanese Agriculture,* Utsonomiya Japan, Bulletin of the Utsonomiya Agricultural College, Vol. 2, No. 1, 1937.

Kawada, S., *"The Establishment and Maintenance of Peasant Farms,"* Kyoto *University Economic Review,* Vol. III, No. 1, July, 1928.

————, "Agricultural Problems and Their Solution in Japan," *Kyoto University Economic Review,* Vol. I, No. 2, December, 1926.

Ladejinsky, Wolf I., *Farm Tenancy in Japan,* Tokyo: General Headquarters, Supreme Commander for the Allied Powers, Natural Resources Section, Report No. 101, 1947.

————, "Trial Balance in Japan," *Foreign Affairs,* October, 1948.

Leonard, Warren H., "Rice as a Crop in Japan," *Journal of the American Society of Agronomy,* Vol. 40, No. 7, July, 1948.

————, *Role of Agriculture in Japan,* (Talk at the University of Wyoming, March 24, 1950).

————, "Principal Field Crops of Japan," *Foreign Agriculture,* Vol. XII, No. 8, August, 1949.

Mukerjee, Radha Kamal, *Land Tenure: India,* Encyclopedia of the Social Sciences, Vol. 9, New York: The Macmillan Co., 1933.

Norman, E. Herbert, *Japan's Emergence as a Modern State,* New York: Institute of Pacific Relations, 1940.

Nasu, Shiroshi, *Aspects of Japanese Agriculture,* New York: Institute of Pacific Relations, 1941.

Raper, Arthur F. and others, *The Japanese Village in Transition,* Tokyo: General Headquarters, Supreme Commander for the Allied Powers, Natural Resources Section, Report No. 136, 1950.

Schumpeter, E. B. and others, *The Industrialization of Japan and Manchukuo, 1930-1940,* New York: The Macmillan Co., 1940.

Sansom, G. B., *Japan, A Short Cultural History,* London: The Cresset Press, 1932.

Sakurai, H., *The Reaction of Landowners in the Kyushu District on the Farmland Reform,* Tokyo: Ministry of Forestry and Agriculture. September, 1947 (typewritten).

Swanson, C. L. W., "Preparation and Use of Composts, Night Soil, Green Manures, and Unusual Fertilizing Materials in Japan," *Agronomy Journal,* Vol. 41, No. 7, July, 1949.

————, "Land Use and Conservation in Japan," *Journal of Soil and Water Conservation,* Vol. 3, No. 40, October, 1948.

Tsuchiya, Takao, *An Economic History of Japan.* Translation of the Asiatic Society of Japan, Second Series, Vol. XV, 1937 (translation by Michitaro Shidehara, revised by Neil Skene).

Trewartha, Glenn Thomas, *Japan A Physical, Cultural & Regional Geography,* Madison: University of Wisconsin Press, 1945.

Takekoshi, Yosaburo, *The Economic Aspects of the History of the Civilization of Japan,* London: George Allen & Unwin Ltd., 1930.

Walworth, Arthur, *Black Ships Off Japan,* New York: Alfred A. Knopf, 1946.

Yoshimoto, Tadasu, *A Peasant Sage of Japan. The Life and Times of Sontoku Ninomiya,* Longmans Green and Co., 1912.

Yagi, Y., "The Problem of Farm Debt Adjustment," *Kyoto University Economic Review,* Vol. XII, No. 1, July, 1937.

————, "The Cooperative Movement Under Wartime Economic Control," *Kyoto University Economic Review,* Vol. XV, No. 3, July, 1940.

————, "The Current Land Problem and the Establishment of Peasant Proprietorship," *Kyoto University Economic Review,* Vol. XI, No. 2, December, 1936.

Standard References, Government Documents, and Statistical Reports

Japanese Agricultural Land Statistics, General Headquarters, Supreme Commander for the Allied Powers, Natural Resources Section, Report No. 101, Tokyo, 1948.

Japanese Army, Notes on Characteristics, Organization, Training, etc. Issued by the General Staff Army Headquarters, Department of the Army, Commonwealth of Australia, Melbourne, January, 1942.

Rural Land Reform. Memorandum for the Imperial Japanese Government. General Headquarters, Supreme Commander for the Allied Powers, December, 1945.

Verbatim Minutes of the Seventh (special) Meeting of the Allied Council for Japan, Tokyo: 17 June 1946.

Corrected Verbatim Minutes of the Thirty-Fifth Meeting Allied Council for Japan, Tokyo: 25 June 1947.

Corrected Verbatim Minutes of the Thirty-Seventh Meeting Allied Council for Japan, Tokyo: 27 July 1947.

Law Concerning the Special Measure for the Establishment of Owner Farmers, Law No. 43, Tokyo: The Official Gazette No. 168 (English Edition), October 26, 1946.

Agricultural Land Adjustment Law revised by Law No. 64 and Law No. 42, Tokyo: The Official Gazette No. 168 (English Edition), October 21, 1946.

The Civil Code of Japan, Tokyo: The International Association of Japan, 1940.

The Japan Year Book 1946-1948, Tokyo: The Foreign Affairs Association of Japan, 1948.

Political Handbook of Japan 1949, Tokyo: The Tokyo News Service Ltd., 1949.

Statistical Year Book of Finance and Economy in Japan 1948, Tokyo: The Ministry of Finance, The Bank of Japan, December, 1948.

Agricultural Programs in Japan 1945-1951, Tokyo: General Headquarters, Supreme Commander for the Allied Powers, Natural Resources Section, Report No. 148, 1951.

Crop Statistics for Japan 1878-1946, Tokyo: General Headquarters, Supreme Commander for the Allied Powers, Natural Resources Section, Report No. 108, 1948.

Japanese Economic Statistics, Bulletin Nos. 33 and 34, Tokyo: General Headquarters, Supreme Commander for the Allied Powers, Economic and Scientific Section, May, June, 1949.

Japanese Natural Resources – A Comprehensive Survey, Prepared in General
Headquarters, Supreme Commander for the Allied Powers. Tokyo: Hosokawa
Printing Company, 1949.